HAWAIIAN JOURNEY

$4.50

Though much of Oahu has become heavily urbanized, there are still areas, particularly on the Windward side, where the old country-style life goes on uninterrupted as seen in this recent photo taken in a Windward valley. In the foreground, a rice paddy.

Alexis H

Dedicated to the loving memory
of Emily Gorham

A view of Honolulu Harbor in 1891. Sailing ships still prevailed but the age of steam was rapidly taking over.

Archives, State of

View of Waikiki and Diamond Head taken in the 1920's.

Archives, State of

Mutual Publishing Company

Copyright ® 1978 by Mutual Publishi
1127 11th Ave., Mezz. B
Honolulu, Hawaii 96816
ISBN 0-935180-04-4
Printed in Taiwan

97 / 98 / 99 / 00 / 01 / 02 / 03 / 0

Preface

Hawaiian Journey originally appeared under the title *Hawaii 1776-1976* to commemorate Hawaii's participation in the Nation's Bicentennial observance. It enjoyed instant popularity among both local residents and visitors to the islands. Now, to reach a wider audience, this completely revised and updated softback edition has been prepared.

Readers who take delight in vintage photographs will find many additional nostalgic pictures, some of which have had only limited circulation. Three new major sections have been included: the tragic story of Princess Kaiulani; the important and recent emergence of what has become known as the Hawaiian Renaissance; and the Neighbor Islands.

Minor sections on the Puerto Ricans and Samoans have also been included to give broader coverage to the multi-ethnicity of Hawaii's population. There has also been some reorganization: the sections entitled Statehood and Islands in Transition have been melded and the previous section on Downtown has been retitled Old Honolulu to permit broader coverage. Throughout the entire book additional narrative has been provided.

In the selection of topics, historical importance was not the sole consideration. The more subjective factor of what makes for interesting storytelling, was given equal weight. The availability of photographs also influenced the selection. However, all the major events and personalities that belong in an overview of Hawaiian history have been included.

The narrative is based on the facts that are available although not everyone may agree with the interpretation. In researching the material it was found that even the experts disagree. Since this is not meant to be a definitive or original work of Hawaiian history, it will not settle any controversy, although the material presented here has been carefully researched.

Hawaiian Journey is intended to serve as a nostalgic introduction to Hawaii's unique story. Hopefully it will contribute to that special pride felt by all who live in these islands.

Along the Oahu Railway at Pearl City, Oahu about 1892.

Robert E. Van Dyke Collection

Table of Contents

Robert E. Van Dyke Col

This photograph, taken in 1872 or 1873 shows the harbor looking back toward the Judiciary Building under construction (the clock is not in yet). All of this area was filled in later years. The new Federal building now stands on this foreground area.

Robert E. Van Dyke Col

The harbor at Kewalo looking toward Diamond Head. This area in later years was filled in and became the site of the U. S. Immigration Station and the Federal Building.

The beach at Makaha, Oahu, 1926.

Robert E. Van Dyke Col

Introduction

Hawaii's history in story and legend is ancient and proud, dating back at least a thousand years before the American colonies became a nation in 1776. It is highly unlikely that the exact date when Polynesian people first set foot on these previously uninhabited islands will ever be known, nor much detail about events occurring between that date and the first contact with Europeans. The Hawaiians were a people without writing, who preserved their history in chants and legends. Much of that early history has disappeared with the death of kahunas and other learned men whose function it was to pass on this knowledge, by means of chants and legends, to succeeding generations.

Modern Hawaiian history begins on January 20, 1778, when Captain James Cook's expedition made its first contact with the Hawaiian people on the islands of Kauai and Niihau. On that day, Hawaii's long isolation from the world beyond its horizons came to an end. So began a most colorful, and sometimes tragic chapter of our nation's history. Certainly it was the most unusual. Beginning with a traditional Polynesian society, Hawaii evolved through an almost bewildering series of cultural and social events that included: nationhood; contact with Western technology and ideas; population decline; massive in-migration of non-Polynesians; overthrow of the Monarchy; a short-lived Republic; annexation as a U.S. Territory; World War II; and statehood.

Although Captain Cook was English, Hawaii's proximity to the U.S. resulted in an early American interest and influence that eventually culminated in statehood. While there were sporadic attempts by the British and the French to bring the islands into their spheres of influence, the American presence was always dominant. American whaling fleets began wintering in Hawaii as early as 1819, and by 1844 as many as 490 American whaling ships crowded Honolulu and Lahaina waters. Protestant missionaries from puritan New England arrived in 1820 to leave a peculiarly American imprint on Hawaii's society and attitudes. At any one time during the Hawaiian monarchy, the majority of foreigners residing in the islands were Americans.

Major events in American history invariably affected Hawaii. The California Gold Rush of 1849 stimulated Hawaiian agriculture, and high prices were paid for Hawaiian sugar, vegetables and meat. Several years later the American Civil War sparked a dramatic expansion of Hawaii's sugar industry to supply the Union when the North was cut off from Southern sugar. The Spanish-American War, from which the U.S. gained bases in the Philippines and Guam, crystalized American military opinion as to Hawaii's strategic central Pacific location. Annexation of Hawaii to the U.S. followed rapidly. The Japanese attack on Pearl Harbor proved a tragic confirmation of Hawaii's strategic value. Today, Hawaii continues to be the nation's bastion of defense in the Pacific.

Because of this early and lasting American influence, Hawaii's social and economic institutions became patterned after those of the U.S., a process accelerated by the fact that significant American contact began at a time when the Hawaiian culture was rapidly disintegrating. Yet there were always differences.

Hawaii's record of assimilating people of different races and nationalities was unequaled by any other State in the Union. Today, about forty percent of the marriages in the State are between people of different races. Hawaii's culture still retains aspects of its Polynesian heritage along with an unmistakeable Oriental influence. The fact that Hawaii is an island group also had an effect. Local lifestyles and values became influenced by the Islands' 3,000 nautical mile isolation from the mainland as well as by the varied ethnic backgrounds and intermingling of its racial groups. As a result, Hawaii's people have always felt unique and different from their mainland cousins.

This sense of uniqueness is now being endangered by rapid economic development, urbanization and increased population growth - all of which now threaten to erode Hawaii's romantic charm and natural beauty. The threat of cultural erosion has permeated Hawaiian history ever since contact with Westerners began. But, if the broad sweep of Hawaiian history suggests anything, it is that the island ways of doing and perceiving things will survive conformist pressures and that Hawaii will retain much of its cherished uniqueness and special way of life.

A photo of an engraving showing the mauka wall of the "Old Fort" on Queen Street.   Archives, State of

The Pali trail near "Honoloulou".   Archives, State of Hawaii

An engraving of a scene near the present site of Kawaiahao Church in 1836.   Archives, State of

View of port Hanarourou, 1816.   The spelling was later changed to Honolulu.

Archives, State of Hawaii

People of the Canoe

Captain Cook was not the first man to "discover" the Hawaiian Islands. He was the first known European to arrive, when he found the Hawaiian archipelago while en route to the North Pacific in search of the Northwest Passage. Cook himself knew that the original Polynesian discoverers of Hawaii had come from the South Pacific hundreds of years before his time.

The language of Hawaii and archaeological discoveries indicate that Hawaii was settled by two distinct waves of Polynesian migration. First, from the Marquesas, came a settlement as early as 600 or 700 AD, and then from the Society Islands, another migration about 1100 AD. After a time of voyaging back and forth, contact with southern Polynesia ceased as the newcomers adapted to their large and lightly-settled islands.

To accomplish long voyages over an immense and lonely sea to thinly scattered islands, the Polynesians developed the technological marvel of the stone age — the seagoing double canoe often reaching between 80 and 100 feet in length. It can more aptly be described as a ship, consisting of two hulls with a platform lashed between to provide living, cooking and work space, and room to transport food, plants and domesticated animals.

The early Polynesians have been called the "Vikings of the Pacific." Without denying the bold seamanship of the intrepid Vikings, the Polynesians were by far their superiors. Lacking instruments of navigation or charts of any kind, the Polynesians sailed into vast oceans. Far from the secure landfalls of nearby continents, they staked their lives on their intimate knowledge of the sky and its stars, the sea and its currents, the flight of birds and many other natural signs.

Plunged for centuries into isolation from the outside world, the Hawaiians developed a unique cultural heritage based on customs brought with them from the south and ways developed in their new land. This was the civilization which Captain Cook found when he burst through the Hawaiian horizon.

Painting by Herb Kawainui Kane © National Geographic Society

The early Polynesians launched immigration and exploring voyages for many reasons. Over-population, loss of a war and famine caused forced voyages, but often the simple desire to seek a new life in a new land was sufficient reason. Herb Kawainui Kane's painting shows Marquesans preparing for such a voyage, loading their ships with prepared foodstuffs, plant cuttings and domestic animals. They will carry supplies for the journey and the basic requirements for continuing their traditional way of life in a new land. The Marquesans, Hawaii's first settlers, were later overwhelmed by newcomers from Tahiti, Bora Bora and Ra'iatea in the Society Islands. The two Polynesian groups melded to produce the unique civilization of Hawaii.

People of the Canoe

People of the Canoe

Painting by Herb Kawainui Kane © National Geographic Society

In 1782, the forces of Chief Kamehameha clashed with those supporting his cousin, Chief Kiwalao, in a decisive power struggle at Mokuohai on the west coast of the Big Island of Hawaii. The greater part of the battle was fought on land but the contending fleets engaged a sizable number of warriors. Kiwalao was killed and his forces defeated, thus clearing the way for Kamehameha's dominion of the island of Hawaii and his eventual unification of all the Hawaiian Islands into one kingdom. Among the battling warriors, a priest raises an image of Kukailimoku, Kamehameha's war god, to direct its power against enemy warriors. This god was aptly named to patronize one who would unite the islands into one nation. Ku-ka-ili-moku means Ku, the snatcher of islands.

Left: Polynesian explorers strike out boldly across unknown seas in search of new land. At least two thousand years of accumulated navigational expertise contributed to their confidence. Their ancestors usually found an island somewhere beyond the horizon, though many an expedition must have perished when land did not appear.

Old Hawaii

In the centuries before the arrival of Captain Cook, Hawaiian society was a highly stratified system with strictly maintained castes. Like medieval Europe and the other Polynesian nations, each caste had its assigned tasks and responsibilities. Not until 1810 was there a single king over all Hawaii. Before then, there were a number of small kingdoms that divided the islands and were often at war with each other.

In each of these small kingdoms, ka moi, the king, headed Hawaii's social pyramid, assisted by a chief minister and a high priest. Next in ranking were the alii or chiefs, who varied in power depending on ancestral lineage and ability. Persons especially trained in the memorization of genealogies were important members of a chief's retinue because a chief's ranking in society was determined by the legitimacy of his genealogy. Chiefs ruled over portions of the land at the whim of the king, who could remove and replace them according to a system of rewards and punishments.

Below the chiefs in temporal power, but often far above them in spiritual power, were the kahuna, or priest craftsmen. They were specialists in professions such as canoe-building, medicine, the casting and lifting of spells, and in other fields. Because of their mysterious powers and supernatural knowledge, the kahuna were feared. They were also highly regarded for their abilities as craftsmen. Though the kahuna held a middle ranking in society, even the highest chiefs treated them with great respect. In addition to their craftsmanship, the kahuna were experts on the religious rites connected with their profession and its patron gods.

The majority of Hawaii's people were commoners (makaainana), subjects of the chief upon whose land they lived. They did most of the hard work: building fishpond walls and housing, fishing, farming, and making tapa cloth. The commoners paid taxes both to the king and to their chief and provided some warriors for the chief's army. These taxes took the form of food, clothing and other products. Unlike medieval serfs, commoners were not bound forever to the territory and ruler. If they wished, they could change allegiance to the chief of another land, but this right was often difficult to exercise.

Below the commoners were a numerically small group of people known as "kauwa" or outcastes. Little is known of their origins or of their true role in Hawaiian society, although they were believed to be slaves of the lowest order.

The "glue" that cemented the ancient social structure was the "kapu" system. The word, known in English as "taboo," meant sacred or prohibited. The daily world of old Hawaii was almost booby-trapped with kapus. Violators were swiftly punished by being strangled or clubbed to death. A commoner had to be careful lest his shadow fall across the person of a high chief, and he had to be quick to kneel or lie down in the presence of such sacred persons. Birth, death, faulty behavior, the building of a canoe, and many other activities were regulated by the kapu system, which permeated all aspects of ancient Hawaiian life.

The Hawaiian temples (heiau) contained images which symbolized the gods. Through prayer and the proper presentation of offerings, the people either sought the help of, or placated the anger of the gods. There were a great number of minor gods associated with all of the occupations but they were mostly variations of the four major gods (who represented the universal forces) known as Ku, Kanaloa, Lono and Kane. Commoners performed their own simple ceremonies to family or personal gods (aumakua) while the complicated religious life of the alii required the services of a kahuna in large temple complexes. In some temples, human sacrifices took place.

Old Hawaii

The woman is beating "wauke" bark to make kapa, which was used for clothing and blankets. Kapa, known also as tapa, can best be described as a kind of soft, pliable paper. Kapa was decorated in various colors using natural plant and shellfish dyes, with geometric designs applied by block-printing. Hawaiians carried the art of kapa decoration to a high state, using more colors and designs than any other Polynesian people. Mats, blankets and a huge old-style wooden surf board lie about the compound. What appears to be a metal bucket may be a sign of encroaching western influence as well as the wooden table and the doorways of the houses, though the artists of the day sometimes took considerable liberties with the facts.

Old Hawaii

"A View in O'whyee, with one of the Priest's Houses." This quaintly titled engraving shows a Hawaiian village scene still untouched by the influence of the outside world. The word "O'whyhee" is one of several attempts to spell "Hawaii" in English before the Hawaiian language was put in written form by a committee of early missionaries. There were no true cities or towns in old Hawaii. People gathered in small coastal villages (kauhale) near good fishing grounds or beside fertile land where they grew taro and sweet potatoes, two main staples of their diet. The better Hawaiian house (hale) was raised on a stone foundation platform and the floor was covered with small smooth pebbles. The homes of commoners had earthen floors covered with dry grasses and lauhala mats.

Old Hawaii

The canoes of fishermen and traveling visitors are drawn up on the beach beside a Hawaiian seaside village. The dim profile of the distant headland suggests that of Diamond Head, thus locating this village in the general area of Waikiki. Most Hawaiian villages were located near the sea. There are some instances of fairly large inland villages, particularly in the uplands of the largest island, Hawaii. But in general, settlements were on the coast. Captain Cook described a Hawaiian village on the island of Kauai as follows: "Though they seem to have adopted the mode of living in villages, there is no appearance of defense, or fortification near any of them; and the houses are scattered about, without any order, either with respect to their distances from each other, or their position in any particular direction. Neither is there any proportion as to their size; some being large and commodious, from forty to fifty feet long, and twenty or thirty broad, while others are mere hovels. Their figure is not unlike oblong corn, or hay-stacks; and they are well thatched with long grass, which is laid on slender poles, disposed with some regularity. The entrance is made indifferently in the end or side, and is an oblong hole, so low, that one must rather creep than walk in; and is often shut up by a board or planks, fastened together, which serves as a door, but having no hinges, must be removed occasionally. No light enters the house, but by this opening; and though such close habitations may afford a comfortable retreat in bad weather, they seem ill-adapted to the warmth of the climate. They are, however, kept remarkably clean; their floors are covered with a large quantity of dried grass, over which they spread mats to sleep upon."

Interior of a Hawaiian chieftain's hut. This engraving was made shortly after western contact with Hawaii when outside influence was still minor. A retainer, carrying a small feather kahili (symbol of nobility) looks after the chief's comfort as household women relax nearby.

A young Hawaiian girl dressed in the traditional "kihei" cape made of tapa. It appears that the Hawaiian tourist industry was off to an early start in depicting the beauty of island girls. This engraving was made in the early decades of the nineteenth century.

Capital punishment in ancient Hawaii. Criminals and violators of kapu were punished by strangulation or clubbing. Sometimes abuses of power took place when an arrogant chief might order the execution of a commoner who displeased him in some way. The fear of sudden and final punishment helped the kahuna and the alii to keep the common people obedient.

Archives, State of Hawaii

John Webber, official artist on Cook's third voyage was interested in recording every possible detail of the new lands and peoples they encountered. This is one of the most unusual recorded sights: a double-hulled sailing canoe manned by masked Hawaiians. The helmet-mask was made of a gourd and the reason for wearing it probably had religious origins.

Left: The Pali, Oahu.

Archives, State of Hawaii

Archives, State of Hawaii

Tattooing was an important art form in most ancient Polynesian societies and in some areas people were heavily tattooed over almost their entire body. Among the Maoris of New Zealand, facial tattooing was extremely complex while among Samoans the decorations were concentrated between the knees and the waist. Tahiti and the Marquesas were among the island groups where the art reached a high state of complexity. The English word tattoo is a direct borrowing from the Marquesan "tatu" or the Tahitian "tatau" by sailors who picked up the word and established it in our vocabulary. The practice of tattooing was less widespread in Hawaii, yet the Hawaiians created numerous designs including birds, plant motifs, and geometric patterns such as the checkerboard style seen on this chieftain. The tattooed words on his arm read "TAMAAHMAH (Kamehameha), died May 8, 1819." Upon the King's death, people throughout the kingdom commemorated the event in the newly learned alphabet. The young man in this drawing was obviously a chieftain because of his large cape, made of thousands of tiny feathers tied in bundles of three to a cord mesh. Such cloaks were a status symbol worn only by high-ranking personages. Additional proof of rank is demonstrated by his feather-covered helmet. Hawaiian helmets resembled those worn by the classical Greeks and Romans.

Captain Cook

Many sea historians believe that Captain James Cook was the greatest seafaring explorer of all time. Born the son of a laborer, he went to sea as an apprentice on a collier in the difficult waters of the North Sea. A competent and cautious navigator, he was painstaking in his calculations and sought constantly to improve his education. He was promoted to Mate at age twenty-four and was in line to become Captain of his own collier. However, upon the outbreak of war with France, he joined the British Navy as an able-bodied seaman. In those days, officers were chosen more for their powerful connections than for their competence. But Cook was an excellent man at whatever task was assigned him and soon he rose to positions of command.

Between 1768 and 1779, Cook commanded three exploring expeditions in the Pacific, ranging from Antarctica to Alaska, Kamchatka to New Zealand and South America. He discovered scores of island groups, surveyed the unknown New Zealand coast, and proved the nonexistence of a hypothetical large continent in the South Pacific.

He came upon Hawaii while enroute to the North Pacific in search of the Northwest Passage. Cook was intelligent and humane. Whenever possible, he attempted peaceful contact with native populations everywhere his expedition touched, even attempting (albeit unsuccessfully) to prevent contact between any of his men who might be diseased and the susceptible island people. Not only was Cook a great navigator, he was also a predecessor of anthropologists, collecting artifacts and recording the peoples, ways of life, and the flora and fauna of new-found lands. He was the first sea captain to prevent scurvy among his crew by insisting on a daily ration of sauerkraut for all hands.

His sweeping searches of the vast Pacific left small blanks to be filled in by later explorers. Captain James Cook was fifty years old when struck down at Kealakekua in the Hawaiian Islands. Today, he might be considered in the prime of life, but by the standards of his harsh and short-lived age, he was an old man. The Hawaiians at Kealakekua innocently honored him as a returned god, but there is no doubt that he was a great man in his own right.

The Resolution and the Discovery, ships of Cook's third voyage, lie at anchor in Kealakekua Bay. Canoes full of curious Hawaiians paddle out to inspect the huge ships and their strange, pale-complexioned crew.

Captain Cook

Captain Cook is deservedly honored for his accomplishments as a navigator and explorer. Strangely, for so famous a man, little is known of his personal life. He was content to let his accomplishments speak for themselves and his journals objectively comment on everything that came into his view while providing little inkling of the deepest thoughts and character of the man himself.

Captain Cook

Archives, State of

On January 16, 1779, Captain Cook's expedition sailed into the sheltering bay of Kealakekua (The Road of the God) on the west coast of the Big Island of Hawaii. The harbor was first explored by Cook's sailing master, a man named Bligh, of later "Mutiny on the Bounty" fame. Cook was unaware that the bay was sacred to Lono, the hero-god who long ago had departed Hawaii from that spot, promising to return some day. Furthermore, January was the time of the Makahiki, a festival in honor of Lono. The sails of the ships resembled the image of Lono so the Hawaiians assumed that the god had returned, true to his ancient promise.

In the engraving, Webber had depicted what he and the rest of the expedition considered was merely an especially fine welcome and honor to their Captain, little realizing just how great an homage was taking place. To the Hawaiians at Kealakekua, Cook was literally the person of the god Lono. In Lono's own heiau (temple) of Hikiau, they draped the bemused Cook with sacred red kapa (tapa cloth), praised him with sacred chants and offered him consecrated pig.

As seen in this engraving and others, the European artists of the time had a tendency toward depicting the Hawaiians as somewhat idealized European types differing only in being darker of complexion. Additionally, in crowd scenes, the same face is seen on every Hawaiian portrayed, perhaps a time-saving device on the part of the artist.

Captain Cook

Captain Cook and his marines moments before the great explorer was killed at Kealakekua Bay in 1779. The unfortunate dispute arose over a stolen cutter and the consequences were deeply regretted by both English and Hawaiians once their passions had subsided.

The romance couldn't last. The Hawaiians welcomed Cook as the god Lono and must certainly have considered his sailors and marines worthy of deference and respect as personal servants of the god. But the personnel of Cook's expedition were all too human, and the Hawaiians were as alert and intelligent as anyone else. They had achieved a remarkably complex life within the limits of a stone-age civilization. The material superiority of the English was the only essential difference between the two peoples. In all other respects they shared the strengths and weaknesses universal to the human condition.

Of all the explorers of that day, Cook was undoubtedly the most humane and thoughtful. He took care to assure the health and happiness of his crew in contrast to the brutal treatment standard in his time. He also made every effort to obtain peaceful contact with newly discovered people, to show them the respect of equals and to observe and report on them as accurately as possible.

The generosity of King Kalaniopuu (King of the island of Hawaii and part of Maui) in provisioning the expedition's ships soon exhausted the produce of the region. The sailors, with their constant demands for food and women began to try the patience of the hospitable Hawaiians and, inevitably, disagreements and provocations arose. They even began to wonder if Cook was a human and not a god.

When the expedition left Kealakekua on February 4, 1779, the weary Hawaiian hosts were much relieved to see what they hoped to be the last of their visitors. Unfortunately, storm gales damaged the *Resolution's* foremast and the expedition returned for repairs. The *Discovery's* cutter was stolen on the night of February 13. The Hawaiians were naturally avid for nails and metal fittings, so superior to wood, stone and bone. Cook and nine marines went ashore and attempted to lure Kalaniopuu aboard Cook's flagship as hostage for the cutter. Meanwhile, because of the theft, the British had blockaded exit from the harbor.

They fired on a canoe attempting to leave the harbor and the outraged Hawaiians counterattacked furiously. Four marines and Cook himself were killed, mute testimony to the great explorer's mortality. Today, a monument marks the spot where Cook was struck down on the shore of Kealakekua. Unfortunately, there is no monument in memory of the Hawaiians who were killed in this bloody conclusion to Hawaii's first contact with Europeans.

Kamehameha I

Born circa 1753 - 1758, Died 1819

King Kamehameha was born in the Hawaiian stone age, a virtually timeless epoch in which the technology of one century differed little, if at all, from that of previous centuries. Yet, by the time of Kamehameha's death, Hawaii's aboriginal culture and neolithic technology were on the verge of extinction. His fledgling kingdom was in the throes of what is today known as "future shock." Each day brought new wonders, new problems, new opportunities and new disappointments.

His birthplace was the Kohala region, northernmost corner of the island of Hawaii. No one knows, nor may ever know the year of his birth, but most experts think that it was some time in the 1750's. As a young man of about twenty-five, he was present at Kealakekua when Captain Cook's ships anchored there.

The young future king was the nephew of Kalaniopuu, king of the Island of Hawaii (and the Hana district of eastern Maui). At the time of Cook's visit, each of the major islands was ruled by a king. Various kings had attempted without success to unite the entire island chain under one command.

In 1780, sickly and sensing that death was near, Kamehameha's aged uncle, King Kalaniopuu, named his oldest son, Kiwalao, as successor. At the same time Kalaniopuu bestowed a high honor on his nephew Kamehameha, selecting him to be the custodian of Kukailimoku, the war god. However exalted this position, Kamehameha was ambitious for higher powers and was not easily placated by this honor. He retired to Kohala, to keep a wary eye on developments until his uncle's death.

When Kalaniopuu died, Kamehameha made his move to settle old scores. The situation gravitated toward open warfare and the deciding battle was fought at Mokuohai where Kiwalao was slain. Kamehameha then proceeded to establish his rule over the entire island of Hawaii. With the Big Island safely in hand, he set out to conquer the leeward islands, moving through Maui, Lanai and Molokai.

To take Oahu, he built an immense fleet of canoes to transport his warriors. They landed in a two-pronged attack with half the fleet coming ashore at Waialae and half at Waikiki. The united force drove Oahu's defenders into Nuuanu Valley, where their defense became a desperate last stand. Trapped in the valley, the Oahuans were forced to surrender or be pushed over the steep Nuuanu Pali.

The conquest of Oahu effectively established the bold and brilliant warrior as lord of all Hawaii. (Recognizing the inevitable, the King of Kauai and Niihau accepted Kamehameha as his sovereign.) Kamehameha proved equally able as a statesman. He united a nation that had never before been united and he kept it together in the face of disruptive foreign and domestic elements.

During Kamehameha's reign Hawaii underwent incredible changes, with the ancient way of life suffering near-lethal blows. Foreign ships arrived in increasing numbers, bringing domestic animals, trees, fruits and plants never before seen in Hawaii. They also brought venereal and other diseases, alcohol and firearms, and carried away young men on their sailing ships. With little immunity to new diseases, the Hawaiians soon began to die in alarming numbers while the destruction of their traditional way of life brought on a melancholy loss of the will to live.

Kamehameha was an old-style autocrat and democracy was foreign to his philosophy. He was equally conservative in religious matters and maintained all the rites, ceremonies and kapus inviolate. Though the common people were losing their respect for the gods as a result of outside impact, the people dared not disrespect them while Kamehameha lived.

Kamehameha brought Hawaii into the modern world as a nation preparing to deal with other nations. From a series of petty and forever-warring chiefdoms, he built a nation. The end of his reign was characterized by long years of peace, a stability previously unknown. For this accomplishment alone, he deserves the title history has bestowed upon him, Kamehameha The Great.

Left: King Kamehameha I, founder of the Hawaiian Kingdom. Though remaining faithful to the gods and customs of old, he was sufficiently pragmatic in adapting western techniques to his needs in unification of the islands into one nation.

Queen Kaahumanu, favorite wife of Kamehameha The Great. A bold and intelligent woman, she served as kuhina-nui (premier) for Kamehameha II and as regent for Kamehameha III. She played a leading role in the overthrow of the ancient kapu system.

Kaahumanu

Born 1772, Died 1832

Queen Kaahumanu was an unusual woman for her time and place. Were she alive today, it is very likely that she would still be considered highly unorthodox. She played a powerful role in the lives of Hawaii's first three kings and, by her actions, several times decided the course of Hawaiian history. Kaahumanu was a complex person endowed with intelligence, wit, audacity and a powerful ambition. A strapping giantess of a woman, she epitomized the old Hawaiian ideal of beauty, which said that bigger was better. This was particularly true of women in the alii class, who were purposely fed a diet that helped increase their generous proportions.

Kaahumanu was the favorite among Kamehameha I's five acknowledged wives. But, she was always a strong-willed woman and her relationship with him was tempestuous. She openly had affairs with other men even after the King, in desperation, had declared a kapu on her body. Death was the penalty for violation of the kapu and at least one chieftain paid with his life for the pleasures of dalliance with the King's wife. At one time, she was very much attracted to another handsome young chief, Kaiana, and when Kamehameha found out about it he was furious. Kaahumanu fled to the home of her parents fearing that the King would beat her violently. Kamehameha loved her despite all but was too proud to ask her to return home. Captain George Vancouver of the British Navy, a good friend of the King, served as a go-between and skillfully arranged the couple's reconciliation.

Kaahumanu bore no children to Kamehameha The Great, but nevertheless managed to dominate two of his sons who successively became kings after his death. At the accession of Kamehameha II, she boldly appropriated half of the new King's power and became the first kuhina-nui, or premier, an office that was held only by women until it was abolished in 1866. She was primarily responsible for the overthrow of the kapu system. In league with the King's mother, Keopuolani, she convinced Kamehameha II to sit down and eat with the women in violation of one of ancient Hawaii's most serious prohibitions.

As a politically ambitious woman, it was in her interest to defy the kapu system, however great the risk. In old Hawaii, women were second-class citizens, more severely handicapped by endless kapus than the men of any class. They were forbidden to eat many delicious foods, they could not eat with their men, and so on. From Kaahumanu's standpoint, the most irksome kapu forbade her to take part in the decision-making councils of the kingdom. Political discussions and machinations took place inside the luakini heiaus (temple enclosures wherein human sacrifices took place) and women were not permitted to enter no matter how exalted their rank. With the overthrow of the kapu system, she was free to exercise her political authority.

When Christian missionaries arrived in 1820, she was cool toward them at first. Later she became a champion of Protestantism, so much so that she expelled French Catholic missionaries and severely strained Hawaii's relations with France.

Though Kamehameha The Great had united the kingdom, Kauai was still semi-independent under a vassal king. Kaahumanu finally consolidated the kingdom by enticing King Kaumualii of Kauai aboard her ship and then sailing off to Honolulu with him. She not only married Kaumualii but also later married his handsome son. Kauai was left with no legal contenders for its throne and Kaahumanu installed her own man as governor.

In 1823, Kamehameha II and Queen Kamamalu died while visiting London and young Kauikeaouli became King Kamehameha III. Kaahumanu served as regent until he reached manhood and continued in her office as kuhina-nui Thus, for a time, she was Hawaii's real ruler. Kamehameha III strongly disagreed with her on the need for stricter enforcement of the law and particularly on the need for any new laws. He was more tolerant of the prevailing lawlessness and laxity of morals whereas Kaahumanu had become rigidly moralistic. Eventually the stubborn kuhina-nui had her way and at least some order was restored to the community.

As she grew older, Kaahumanu became more religious, to the point of zealousness and intolerance. She kept Hawaii Protestant while she lived and other sects prospered only after her death. She died in 1832, a remarkable woman by any standard and a great woman in the history of Hawaii.

Kamehameha II

Born 1797, Died 1824

It is hard to imagine a greater contrast in characters than the one between young Liholiho (Kamehameha II) and his father, Kamehameha I. Where the great King had been firm, his son wavered; where the father was strong, the son was weak. Liholiho was not the most suitable king for his time.

Liholiho was twenty-two years old when he became King at Kailua-Kona on May 20, 1819. Hardly had he been sworn in before the gathered chieftains of his realm, than he demonstrated the weakness and vacillation that were to characterize his reign. Kaahumanu, his father's favored wife, confronted the new King in front of the assembled nobles and said that it had been his father's wish for her to share rulership of the land. Had any-

one attempted such audacity in front of Kamehameha I, the culprit might well have been slain on the spot. Liholiho, offering no objection, split his power in half by accepting Kaahumanu as kuhina-nui, a newly invented title meaning premier, but which implied the sharing of kingly power.

Always unsure of his power, the fledgling King allowed a further dissipation of kingly prerogative by submitting to the demand of the chiefs that the royal sandalwood monopoly be turned over to them.

Early in Liholiho's reign an event of major proportions within the context of traditional Hawaiian society took place. The event was preceded by incessant pressures on the King initiated by Kaahu-

manu and Keopuolani, his mother. One day at a feast in Kailua, and after much hesitation and deliberation, Liholiho sat down to eat with a group of noble women in view of onlooking commoners. It was a serious matter, for his power and that of the alii was bolstered by the kapu system. The effect was electrifying. The King himself was openly violating one of the most sacred of all kapus, that which prohibited men and women from eating together. The signal had unmistakably been given that the ancient religion of Hawaii was dying. Shortly thereafter, Liholiho ordered god images burned and heiaus demolished throughout the islands. The ancient social fabric was to become rent beyond repair.

Kamehameha II was a restless man, constantly roaming about. Perhaps he was unconsciously fleeing from the problems and responsibilities of his office, for it was a time of great changes and he was unable to cope with them. With his escapist nature, it was inevitable that he would one day venture to the world beyond Hawaii.

On November 27, 1823, Kamehameha II boarded a chartered ship along with his Queen Kamamalu and a few chiefs and women and sailed to England. The Hawaiian entourage toured London, attended the theater and joined the merriment at parties and entertainments arranged in their honor by the British aristocracy. A formal audience with King George IV had to be cancelled when both the King and Queen contracted measles, a disease to which the Hawaiians had little immunity. Queen Kamamalu died on July 8, 1824, and the despondent King Kamehameha II followed her on July 14. Their bodies were returned to Hawaii aboard H.M.S. Blonde of the British Navy, commanded by Captain The Lord Byron, cousin of the famed poet.

Archives, State of Hawaii

Kamehameha III

Born 1814, Died 1854

Archives, State of Hawaii

King Kamehameha III ruled Hawaii longer than any other monarch and guided the kingdom through a difficult period of transition. The Hawaiians called him "Ka Mo'i Lokomaika'i", The Benevolent King.

Kauikeaouli, the last son of Kamehameha The Great to rule, ascended the throne of Hawaii when he was ten years old, upon the death of his older brother Liholiho (King Kamehameha II) in London. Kuhina-nui Kaahumanu governed as regent during Kauikeaouli's boyhood with the assistance of a council of chiefly advisors. His reign of twenty-nine years was the longest of any Hawaiian monarch.

Kauikeaouli was king at a most difficult period in Hawaii's history. The influx of large numbers of foreign residents brought new problems concerning trade, credit, land titles and a plague of complications unknown to the simple Hawaii of just a few generations earlier. At a time when traditional Hawaiian social restraints had broken down, the prevailing lawlessness provoked difficulties with foreign countries, particularly Great Britain.

Nevertheless, Kamehameha III brought his kingdom safely through a long reign full of difficulties. Although he yearned for a return to old ways, he instituted progressive measures for the good of his people. In his lifetime, Hawaii moved from autocracy toward democracy and from kingship to constitutional monarchy.

King Kamehameha III died in Honolulu on December 15, 1854, after having named his nephew, Alexander Liholiho, as successor. Kauikeaouli served Hawaii long and to the best of his ability and conscience. That he was beloved by his people is his epitaph in Hawaiian history.

Kamehameha III

Prince Kauikeaouli   Robert E. Van Dyke Collection

Princess Nahienaena   Robert E. Van Dyke Col

During his young manhood, personal troubles worthy of a Greek tragedy embittered his life. Prince Kauikeaouli and his sister, Princess Nahienaena, were very much in love. Shocking as this may seem to modern Western sensibilities, such unions were acceptable among the nobles of ancient Hawaii, just as they were among the Egyptian pharaohs. Close relatives often married to keep the chiefly bloodlines pure and to assure children with powerful "mana." This word describes a Polynesian concept in which certain persons possess supernatural power and authority derived from ancestors who held mana. It could be accumulated by uniting persons or families with powerful mana; the offspring being even more charged with the divine electricity than their parents. The greater the charge of mana a person was endowed with, the greater his sacred power. Tortured by love for her brother and guilt from new-found Christian beliefs that had made inroads into traditional Hawaiian ways, Princess Nahienaena drifted into despondency and died at the age of twenty-one. Long after Prince Kauikeaouli became King Kamehameha III, he regularly visited her grave in Lahaina.

Kamehameha IV

Born 1834, Died 1863

Alexander Liholiho succeeded his uncle, Kamehameha III, on December 15, 1854, taking the title of Kamehameha IV. He was the first grandson of Kamehameha The Great to become King of Hawaii.

During Kamehameha IV's reign and that of his successor, there was a growing agitation on the part of the sugar planters for annexation to the United States to secure a dependable market for their product. At the same time, the Hawaiian monarchs sought to strengthen their own power and carry out a policy of "Hawaii for the Hawaiians." Within the Hawaiian government there was continuous wrangling between those who were interested in strengthening the power of the throne and those who wished to limit that power and extend democracy to the citizenry. Many foreign residents did not wish to become citizens of Hawaii but wanted to be able to vote in elections. They wanted political power to safeguard their interests and would have preferred that common Hawaiians remain voteless.

When Alexander was still a 15-year-old prince, Finance Minister Gerrit Judd took him and his brother, Lot, on a European trip designed to further their education as future monarchs and to settle some differences that had soured relations between France and the Hawaiian Kingdom. While in France, the young Princes were entertained by the highest elements of society and met with Emperor Louis Napoleon.

In 1856, Kamehameha IV married the beautiful Emma Rooke, a part-European descendant of Hawaiian chieftains and granddaughter of an Englishman. A cultivated and witty pair, Alexander and Emma came to symbolize all that was elegant, stylish and artistic. Though they brought many non-Hawaiian advisors into the government, they were careful to limit missionary participation. King Kamehameha IV was one of the most anti-American of all Hawaii's monarchs and he showed a marked preference for the British from an early age.

The royal pair became the proud parents of Prince Albert, a bright and handsome little boy who was the apple of their eye and the hope of the Kamehameha dynasty. Unfortunately, tiny Prince Albert died when only four years old and the king never really recovered from this shattering blow to his love and hopes. Fifteen months later, on November 30, 1863, Alexander Liholiho died. After his death, Queen Emma attempted once more to become a monarch. In 1874, her candidacy for Queen was considered by the Hawaiian Legislature but David Kalakaua was elected.

Archives, State of Hawaii

Kamehameha V

Born 1830, Died 1872

Lot Kamehameha, as King Kamehameha V, was the final direct descendant of Kamehameha The Great to sit on Hawaii's throne and the last Hawaiian monarch to reign in the old style. After him, Hawaii's rulers were elected by the Hawaiian Legislature — a progressive step for those of a democratic frame of mind but anathema to aristocratic believers in the "divine right" of kings.

Lot was a true descendant of Kamehameha I in more ways than one. Throughout his reign Kamehameha V opposed any erosion of royal power and he oversaw the adoption of a new constitution designed to strengthen the royal hand. He was a more truly Hawaiian king than his younger brother Alexander (Kamehameha IV). While Alexander had been worldly and witty, graceful and elegant, Lot was stolid, and more of a nativist in every respect.

Problems with the United States continued vexsome as they had during his brother's reign. Agitation by certain elements in favor of annexation by the U.S. threatened Hawaii's independence. The King, in an effort to defuse relations between the two countries, promoted a treaty of reciprocity that would allow Hawaiian sugar to enter the American market duty-free. The Civil War had cut the Union off from Southern sugar and so there was a great demand from the North for sugar. Until this time, Hawaii had depended heavily on the whaling fleets as a source of income. By the end of the 1850's whaling was in a gradual decline and was no longer a strong economic force in the islands

Racial troubles increased in Lot's era due to well-founded suspicions that the whites were trying to take over the kingdom. In 1866, a fist fight broke out in the Legislature between white and Hawaiian members. Such an incident was probably long overdue for it was a most peculiar legislature wherein white legislators refused to speak Hawaiian, the kingdom's official language, and native Hawaiian members understandably refused to use English.

King Lot Kamehameha was in bad health for several years before his death. For some unknown reason, he never discussed the matter of succession, though it was of vital importance since he had never married and had no children. As he lay on his deathbed, his counselors and advisors mentioned at least five eminently eligible candidates, all of then high-ranking alii men and women. Lot died on December 1, 1872, his forty-second birthday, without naming a successor, thus ending the dynasty founded by Kamehameha The Great. From then on, Hawaii's monarchs would be elected.

Archives, State of Hawaii

Lunalilo

Born 1835, Died 1874

William Lunalilo was confirmed as King of Hawaii by the Hawaiian Legislature after an informal popular vote. He took his oath of office at Kawaiahao Church on January 12, 1873.

Only two of the five possible candidates for the monarchy campaigned seriously — David Kalakaua, chieftain from a line distantly related to the Kamehamehas, and William Charles Lunalilo, descended from one of the half-brothers of Kamehameha The Great. Although Lunalilo won, Kalakaua was soon to take over because King Lunalilo ascended the throne with an advanced tubercular affliction.

Lunalilo was a personally charming man with a taste for music, literature and the arts. Lunalilo is known to have drunk too much for a man in his weakened condition. Among the common Hawaiian people his "weakness" was hardly considered worthy of comment. They loved him and would have forgiven him for far worse than a penchant for alcoholic drinks.

Lunalilo was more liberal than his predecessor, and made serious efforts to democratize the constitution. Once again, during his short reign, the question of a treaty of reciprocity with the U.S. arose. The Hawaiian sugar industry needed a natural market like the United States to absorb its increasing production. This time, the question of the treaty was linked with the suggestion of ceding Pearl Harbor to the United States in exchange for favorable terms.

King Lunalilo allowed himself to endorse the cession of Pearl Harbor, though he felt it was an unwise accommodation to the powerful American giant. Once the news reached the Hawaiian public, they were outraged. They could readily understand that a treaty of reciprocity could be of economic benefit to the kingdom, but to cede Hawaiian land to a foreign power! Widespread disapproval of the idea forced its eventual abandonment.

One of the most personally humiliating events of Lunalilo's short reign was the mutiny of the Royal Household Troops. This numerically small body of soldiers had long chafed under the excessively harsh discipline of the senior officers who, to make matters worse, were white foreigners. The mutiny was put down only by a personal plea from the King himself, guaranteeing amnesty for all participants.

It must have been a difficult and embarrassing moment, demonstrating all too clearly the low estate to which Hawaii's monarchy had fallen. Afterwards, the Royal Household Troops were disbanded and the Kingdom was left without a standing army, a factor which later helped contribute to the success of those who overthrew the monarchy.

King Lunalilo died on February 3, 1874. His reign had lasted only slightly more than a year. Like his predecessor, he failed to name a successor and the question would be decided by the incoming Legislature of 1874.

Archives, State of Hawaii

Kalakaua

Born 1836, Died 1891

King David Kalakaua was elected by the Hawaiian Legislature of 1874 amid scenes of violence and indignity. His rival for the throne was the dowager Queen Emma. What her followers lacked in numbers they made up for in willingness to make trouble.

Kalakaua was concerned with the well-being of his native Hawaiian people. He maintained a policy of filling administrative posts with Hawaiians wherever possible, a practice that did little to calm the fears of American businessmen who had supported him against Queen Emma. While naturally favoring his people, Kalakaua repeatedly and sincerely insisted that there was room in Hawaii for all kinds of people

The new king soon proved himself a hard-headed individualist with unpredictable ways. He fired cabinet members and ministers when they disagreed with him and his powerful ego sometimes involved him in questionable schemes of a grandiose nature. At one time he envisioned himself as a sort of Polynesian emperor, dreaming of a Federation of Pacific Islands with Hawaii at its head, and, of course, himself at the helm. He began meddling in the affairs of Samoa, going so far as to obtain the Samoan King's (Malietoa) signature on an agreement of federation. But at the time, Samoa was having trouble with imperialists from Germany, the U.S. and England

Archives, State of

and the Hawaiian negotiations were unsuccessful.

In late 1882, when the new Iolani Palace was completed, Kalakaua decided that such a magnificent stage deserved an equally magnificent performance. On February 12, 1883, he held a coronation ceremony during which he crowned himself King in the manner of Napoleon. Though much of the ceremonial was borrowed from European protocol, Kalakaua attempted to blend it with Hawaiian traditions, including mass dances of the ancient sacred hulas.

King Kalakaua became known in Hawaiian history as the "Merry Monarch." He loved parties, balls and entertainments. He enjoyed talking to such noted visitors as Robert Louis Stevenson.

Toward the end of his reign, Kalakaua suffered various setbacks to his power. His cabinet was overthrown. A new constitution that deprived him of almost all his power was written and in July 1889, an ill-fated insurrection took place under elements favoring the abdication of Kalakaua and his replacement by Princess Liliuokalani. In November, 1890, because of declining health, Kalakaua went to California to recuperate, leaving Liliuokalani as regent in his stead. He suffered a stroke and died on January 20, 1891, in San Francisco at the age of fifty-four.

Iolani Palace

Little imagination is required to picture the last home of Hawaii's monarchs, Iolani Palace, filled with nobles, ministers and officials, dressed in fancy uniforms attending gala balls and accompanied by beautiful ladies in elegant gowns. Iolani is a sacred name meaning "Royal Hawk" in the Hawaiian language. The hawk, flying high above other birds, was a symbol of royalty.

The present rococo and gingerbread fairy-tale building is actually the second Iolani Palace to stand on the site. The first, a much less impressive cottage-like structure, was constructed in 1845. Its first occupant was King Kamehameha III. By the time King David Kalakaua ascended the throne, the old palace was no longer considered a fitting residence for a king and it was torn down to be replaced by the present Iolani Palace.

Construction of the present Iolani Palace was completed in 1882. The basic construction was of brick, cement and concrete block. Its architecture was a composite of several styles designed to capture the mood of Hawaiian monarchy in the late 1800's.

The palace did not serve long as a residence for royalty. Eleven years after its completion, the monarchy was overthrown by the Provisional Government which preceded the Republic of Hawaii and its later annexation to the United States. Here, Queen Liliuokalani was held for nine months as a political prisoner, during which time she wrote many of the lovely songs which have come down to this day.

After annexation, Iolani Palace remained the center of Hawaiian government under the Territory and State. The State Senate met in the former royal dining room and the throne room seated the House of Representatives. This situation continued until the completion of a new State Capitol in 1968. Today, Iolani Palace has undergone a complete renovation to restore its original splendor.

Archives, State of Hawaii

Officers and retainers of the Royal Court pose on the verandah of Iolani Palace. Three attendants hold kahili, feather standards symbolizing nobility.

25

Princess Liliuokalani who would later become Queen. An imperious monarch, she was determined to gain back the royal power her brother, King Kalakaua, had lost. Her impetuosity brought about the clash with annexationists which resulted in the downfall of the monarchy. She is best known to the world beyond Hawaii as the composer of the beloved and beautiful "Aloha Oe."

Liliuokalani

Born 1838, Died 1917

Liliuokalani was already leading the nation as regent when King Kalakaua died in San Francisco. At the time that she became Queen, the political and economic climate was extremely complicated. Rivalry was intense between white businessmen who dominated the economy and native politicians who still retained the power to get things accomplished.

The possibility of annexation to the United States was being openly discussed by representatives of the business community and the "better" classes. Many citizens were taking actions that could best be described as treasonous. The annexationists were badly outnumbered, and certainly the majority of the Hawaiian people, as well as many white residents, were against annexation. But the economic power structure was not intimidated by mere lack of popular support. On the whole, these businessmen were those who considered Hawaiians incapable of self-government. And, as businessmen, the annexationists believed that the monarchy was too inept to safeguard the interests of property and profits.

Tension grew when the Queen announced her intention to promulgate a new constitution which would restore the power of the monarchy, much of which had been lost in 1887 under a constitution signed by King Kalakaua. Even members of her own cabinet were alarmed and disapproving, fearing that it would give the annexationists the ammunition they sought. Her efforts caused that reaction.

A Committee of Safety was formed by the prominent annexationists. They took it upon themselves to create a provisional government and a militia. The Queen could have declared martial law and arrested the conspirators, but she felt that this would begin armed conflict which would result in loss of innocent lives. Although the Queen did not act, the Committee of Safety made its move and armed companies of militia took over government buildings and offices. The evening before, marines and sailors from the U.S.S. Boston were landed to keep order in Honolulu and their commander, Captain G. C. Wiltse, openly supported the Provisionals. The Queen was powerless.

She asked the U.S. minister to support her sovereignty, but he replied that in his opinion the Provisional Government was now the only legal government in Hawaii. Finally, just after sunset on January 17, 1893, the Queen faced the inevitable and surrendered under protest. On January 31, Minister Stevens, at the request of the Provisional Government's advisory council, raised the U.S. flag over Honolulu. Annexation was thought to be a mere formality. However, President Cleveland sent a special investigator to Hawaii in March 1893 with instructions to investigate the situation and to determine what had actually taken place. Much to the chagrin of the Provisionals, President Cleveland's administration concluded that the monarchy had been overthrown by force with the complicity of the U.S. minister. The Provisional Government refused to step down and the U.S. refused to annex Hawaii. In any case, Liliuokalani's reign as Queen of Hawaii had ended. Though disheartened by Washington's rejection, the Provisionals stepped ahead boldly and established the Republic of Hawaii on July 4, 1894, with Sanford Dole as President.

In 1895, Hawaiians loyal to the Queen staged a revolt in an attempt to restore Liliuokalani to the throne. The revolt was soon crushed and the Queen was arrested and placed under detention in an apartment of Iolani Palace. She also was forced to relinquish any claim to the throne as a condition to obtain amnesty for the Hawaiian rebels.

The Spanish-American War in 1898 precipitated American reconsideration of its position on Hawaii. The U.S. had taken over the Philippines and Hawaii's strategic value was now obvious. President McKinley signed the resolution of annexation on July 7, 1898. It may have been a happy day for the businessmen and new ruling classes of Hawaii, but for many others it was a day of sadness. Large numbers of royalists and common Hawaiians gathered quietly at the home of deposed Queen Liliuokalani and Crown Princess Kaiulani to silently console them and pay homage to the last monarch of the forever-lost kingdom. On June 14, 1900, Hawaii formally became a Territory under an Organic Act, and Sanford Dole, who had served as President of the Hawaiian Republic, was sworn in as Hawaii's first Territorial Governor.

As a young princess, the future Queen married John Dominis who had inherited Washington Place, located behind Iolani Palace. After the overthrow of her government, Liliuokalani resided there until her death in 1917. She is best known to the outside world as the composer of that lovely and haunting song that evokes Hawaii wherever it is heard—"Aloha Oe."

Though she was legally known as Lydia Dominis after her forced abdication, the people of Hawaii called her Queen Liliuokalani as long as she lived, and this is her name to Hawaiians today.

The Republic of Hawaii

Officers of the Provisional Government of Hawaii after the overthrow of the Monarchy and shortly before the establishment of the short-lived Republic which was followed by U.S. Annexation. Shown here are (l. to r.), James A. King, Sanford B. Dole (president of the Republic and first Territorial governor), William O. Smith and Peter C. Jones.

THE PACIFIC
Commercial Advertiser.

Established July 2, 1856.

VOL. XXVIII., NO. 4971.   HONOLULU, HAWAIIAN ISLANDS, THURSDAY, JULY 14, 1898.   PRICE FIVE CENTS.

ANNEXATION!

"HERE TO STAY!"

And the star-spangled banner
In triumph shall wave,
O'er the Isles of Hawaii
And the homes of the brave.

—H. M. WHITNEY.

FIRST NEWS.

HONOLULU, H. I., U. S. A., July 13, 1898, 3:30 p. m.—The Pacific Mail S.S. Coptic signals from off Waikiki that these Islands have been annexed to the United States by the passage in the Senate at Washington of the House Joint Resolution.

Flags are being hoisted everywhere.

Thousands flocked to the water front.

There are great crowds on the streets evidencing the very delirium of joy.

At 4:15 a salute of 100 guns was fired.

At 4:20 all the whistles were sounding.

VOTE AT WASHINGTON.

WASHINGTON, July 6.—With a rush, without the change of a word, the resolutions which make Hawaii a part of the United States were passed by the Senate this afternoon. From out of a situation which gave no promise of ending for weeks, perhaps, and at a time when those who have had charge of the filibuster against the measure had been assuring every one that they could not see a vote for a week, there came a demand for a roll call on the first amendment of the list of eight which had to be disposed of before the main question could be considered. Senator White almost surprised himself when he shut off debate, ended the filibuster which has prevented the acceptance of the Hawaiian resolution and gave the majority of the Senate a chance to express its will.

An agreement was reached partly last night and partly this morning, but has been in sight for several days. The Republican leaders had been hard at work for two days in their endeavor to blockade the windward passage of the anti-annexation filibuster. They succeeded when they showed the utter inability of the Democrats to keep up their performance sufficiently long to have any effect whatever. Not more than 22 votes against the resolution could be counted by the most sanguine, while the annexationists' forty-five was still intact.

and the Congress of the Islands. It is believed that this will be done by a special messenger, probably John W. Foster, former secretary of State, and that the cruiser Philadelphia will carry the messenger to the Islands.

Immediately upon the passage by the Hawaiian Congress of an act which makes effective the Newlands resolution the commissioner will raise the American flag and the Philadelphia will salute it.

It is believed that the commission which will be sent to the islands to frame the laws for their future government will be

DR. JOHN S. McGREW.
"Father of Annexation"
(Photo by Williams)

treaty which has never been ratified, but is now pending in the Senate of the United States."

Pettigrew then offered his amendment to repeal the contract labor laws now in force on the Hawaiian Islands. It was rejected—41 to 22.

Bacon of Georgia offered an amendment providing that the annexation resolutions should not be operative until they had been approved by a majority of the electors of Hawaii. Defeated—20 to 42.

Faulkner of West Virginia offered an amendment providing that the duties of the civil, judicial and military powers shall be exercised under authority of existing laws not in conflict with the Constitution and laws of the United States. Rejected—20 to 43.

Allen offered an amendment placing an internal revenue tax of 1 cent a pound on Hawaiian sugar. It was defeated, 57 to 4, the four voting for the amendment being Allen Morrill, McEnery and Pettigrew.

Pettigrew offered an amendment that all native-born male Hawaiians over 21 years of age and all naturalized aliens shall be allowed to vote in the

CERVERA'S FLEET IS ANNIHILATED

Attempted to Run the Blockade at Santiago.

He Is a Prisoner---Heavy Losses.

CERVERA'S FLEET WIPED OUT.

WASHINGTON, JULY 4.—The following bulletin from Commodore Watson was received to-night:

PLAYA DEL ESTE, July 3.—To the Secretary of the Navy:

COMMANDER W. S. SCHLEY.
Commodore Winfield Scott Schley first attracted the attention of the world in 1884, when he was put in command of the expedition sent to the Arctic for the relief of the Greeley exploration party. He also had a part in the Chilian trouble in 1891, as commander of the Baltimore.

At 9:30 a. m. today the Spanish squadron, seven in all, including one gunboat, came out of Santiago harbor in columns and was totally destroyed within an hour, excepting the Cristobal Colon, which was chased forty-five miles to the westward by the commander-in-chief, the Brooklyn, the Oregon, and the Texas, surrendering to the Brooklyn, but was beached to prevent sinking.

None of our officers or men were injured except on board the Brooklyn. Chief Yeoman Ellis was killed and one man wounded.

Admiral Cervera, all the commanding officers, excepting of the Oquendo, about 70 other officers and 1600 men are prisoners. About 350 were killed or drowned and 160 wounded. The latter are cared for on the Solace and the Olivette.

WATSON.

29

A Strange Reunion

If Sanford B. Dole (left), former president of the short-lived Republic of Hawaii, and Liliuokalani, former Queen of the Kingdom of Hawaii, seem less than pleased on the occasion of this photograph, they have good reason. Dole was instrumental in the forceful overthrow which brought an end to the Hawaiian monarchy and later subjected the Queen to the humiliation of house arrest in an apartment in her own Iolani Palace. Each felt that they were correct and perfectly justified in the actions taken at the time. Perhaps in the twenty years that had passed before this gathering was recorded they had resumed their original friendship. If they had, it certainly does not show by the grim looks on their faces. This meeting was arranged by Henry Berger (standing), leader of the Royal Hawaiian Band for forty years. Berger arranged the meeting in the interests of patriotic solidarity and to elicit public support of American aid to the Allied cause in World War I. Certainly neither Dole nor the former Queen could be overjoyed at the idea of meeting, but each may have felt that this public meeting would evoke good feelings on the part of all Hawaiian citizens. The nervously uncomfortable observer on the right was the Governor of the Territory of Hawaii, Lucius E. Pinkham.

Young Princess Kaiulani.

Archives, State of Hawaii

Archives, State of Hawaii

Kaiulani in the days when she was the last hope of the kingdom soon to be lost.

31

Princess Kaiulani

Her story is one of romance and tragedy, the short life of a beautiful princess whose kingdom was stolen away from her. Of all the events connected with the overthrow of the Hawaiian Monarchy, the most touching concern this lovely heiress to a throne that ceased to exist while she was preparing herself to occupy it.

Kaiulani was born October 16, 1875, the daughter of Princess Miriam Likelike and Archibald Cleghorn, a prominent Honolulu businessman born in Edinburgh, Scotland. On Christmas Day of the same year, in St. Andrew's Cathedral, she was christened Victoria Kawekiu Lunalilo Kalaninuiahilapalapala Kaiulani. A descendant of the highest Hawaiian alii, her uncle King David Kalakaua ruled Hawaii when she was born and later, her Aunt Liliuokalani was to become the last Queen of Hawaii. King Kalakaua was particularly overjoyed at her birth. Childless himself, he was happy to know that his sister had produced an heir to the throne to follow Liliuokalani.

Princess Kaiulani spent a happy childhood at her family's home in Waikiki. A beautiful estate surrounded by lush gardens and walkways, it was called Ainahau, meaning "cool place" in the Hawaiian language. It was an idyllic existence, with the house always full of interesting people and her parents were well liked by Hawaiians and non-Hawaiians. But, the tragedies that were to form Kaiulani's character began to strike at an early age. Her mother, Princess Likelike, became ill in December 1886 and her formerly outgoing nature became quiet and withdrawn. On the afternoon of February second, 1887, Likelike died at the age of thirty-seven, leaving behind a distraught husband and an inconsolable twelve-year old daughter. The family home at Ainahau, after a period of mourning, continued to be one of the most popular settings for Honolulu's elite. Perhaps the most interesting visitor of all, from the young princess's viewpoint, was Robert Louis Stevenson who sailed into Honolulu Harbor in January 1889. He became friends with King Kalakaua who introduced him to Kaiulani and her father. Stevenson was thoroughly captivated by the beautiful young Scots-Hawaiian princess. The fascination was mutual and they spent long hours conversing together under the large banyan tree that stood in front of the house at Ainahau.

When she became thirteen, it was felt the Kaiulani should have an education befitting a future occupant of the Hawaiian throne. She became the first member of the Hawaiian royalty to receive the kind of training traditionally given to the children of European monarchs in preparation for ascending to the throne.

Princess Kaiulani sailed to England, via San Francisco, in 1889 and it was to be eight long years before the lovely young woman returned to her native islands. During her stay in Europe, she traveled widely and was taught French, German, literature and other subjects, including the social graces expected of one in her high position.

With each passing year her beauty grew and matured and she soon became a very popular young woman, pursued by eligible bachelors from the nobility and upper stratas of European society. Though she was a high spirited and vivacious girl, she never took any of her suitors seriously, concentrating more on preparation for the destiny that awaited her at home.

But the news from home became more puzzling and ominous with each passing day, beginning with a letter from her uncle King Kalakaua who warned enigmatically that she be on guard against enemies. This was to be the last letter from the King to Kaiulani. He died in San Francisco on January 20, 1891 while consulting with physicians over his deteriorating health.

The King's sister, Liliuokalani, next in line for the throne, became the reigning monarch and Kaiulani was now the Crown Princess. Liliuokalani's reign was short-lived and she had to deal with treachery at every turn, as prominent businessmen and even members of her own cabinet plotted against her.

In January of 1893, Kaiulani was to hear that the Monarchy had been overthrown and that a Provisional Government had taken power. This bad news had its effect on the vulnerable young princess and her health began to falter under the pressure. She was homesick to begin with and increasingly felt that she belonged back in Hawaii where she could at least take part in events and help her people, who had been taken over by a government that did not represent their aspirations.

Princess Kaiulani journeyed to Washington and sought an audience with President Cleveland to plead the cause of the legitimate Monarchy against the usurpers of the Provisional Government who, at the same time were busily lobbying for annexation by the U.S. government. The gentle and aristocratic bearing of the exotically beautiful princess captivated the American public which in general sympathized with her plight. The President appointed a commissioner to investigate the situation in Hawaii, an action which frustrated the Provisionals for many months.

Having done what she could, Kaiulani returned to Europe to resume her studies. She came home to Hawaii in 1897.

Princess Kaiulani

Although the Royalist cause was desperate, the fight continued. Hawaiians referred to Kaiulani as "Our Last Hope." Finally, in 1898, Hawaii was annexed to the United States and Kaiulani's right to become Queen of her nation was lost for all time.

Kaiulani went through the motions of living but something seemed to have gone out of her. She still attended the round of luaus and parties and outings that were her lot as a popular princess, but her former vitality had disappeared. Her attitude became increasingly fatalistic and she seemed to have nothing to live for.

More and more she sought to get away from Honolulu with its atmosphere of swaggering American soldiers and the arrogance of the new government. In December, 1898, Kaiulani accepted an invitation to attend a wedding at the Parker Ranch in the cool uplands of the northern part of the Big Island of Hawaii. She had always loved horseback riding and here she could indulge this pleasure at will. With a defiance that had become part of her character since the downfall of the Monarchy, and against the advice of her friends, Kaiulani went riding once too often in the chilly wind and rain. For some time her health had been fragile and soon she came down with a fever.

She did not improve and was brought back to Honolulu by ship. In her home at Ainahau the doctors diagnosed her condition as rheumatism of the heart complicated by other symptoms. After a lingering illness, Princess Kaiulani died on March sixth, 1899, surrounded by her heartbroken father, friends and relatives. Thus passed, at only twenty-three years, a beautiful fairytale princess, Hawaii's "Last Hope." With her death a romantic era faded into the mist of the past. Hawaii entered the matter-of-fact, coldly realistic 20th century.

As a mature woman Kaiulani's beauty bewitched all who saw her.   Archives, State of Hawaii

Missionaries Asa and Lucy Goodale Thurston. This ambrotype was taken on October 12, 1859 on their 40th wedding anniversary.

Above: Sereno Edwards Bishop, first missionary born in Hawaii at Kaawaloa on February 7, 1827. This portrait was taken upon the occasion of his graduation from Amherst College in Massachusetts in the year 1846.

Above Right: Mrs. Maria Sartwell Loomis, wife of Elisha Loomis, the first printer in Hawaii. She bound the first books west of the Rocky Mountains about 1850.

A missionary family of the mid-1800's. Reverend Samuel C. Damon and his family administered to the seamen who crowded the port of Honolulu. Many of the early missionary portraits are of elderly people, but it must be remembered that many of them arrived in Hawaii as young people long before the invention of photography. Even then, it was to be many years before photography became popular. In a way, the early missionaries were a sort of Peace Corps of their time, imparting technological skills along with their basic religious message.

Edwin Oscar Hall and Sarah Lyon Williams Hall who were stationed in Honolulu in 1835.

Missionaries

An anti-missionary adage still current in the islands says of the missionaries, "They came to do good, and did well." Certainly many missionary descendants

Robert E. Van Dyke Collection

An early portrait of the sisters, Sarah Eliza Peirce and Harriet Peirce (standing). Sarah married Nathaniel Bright Emerson, the first doctor born in Hawaii. Sarah went on to become the first woman doctor to practice in Hawaii.

used their connections and influence to gain advantages in business and in obtaining large grants of land. Nevertheless, the original missionaries lived spartan lives of dedication, hard work and self-sacrifice. To them the epigram does a disservice.

The missionaries can hardly be blamed for the destruction of the Hawaiian religion. When they arrived in Hawaii in 1820, prepared to do battle "against the forces of heathenish idolatry," the Hawaiian people had already dismantled their heiaus and had rejected their religious beliefs. One can imagine the surprise with which the missionaries received this unexpected bit of good news.

From 1837 to 1840, nearly 20,000 Hawaiians accepted Christianity. Having rejected their own religion a generation earlier, the Hawaiian people were in no hurry to accept a new one. They observed the detrimental effects of many of the new foreign influences. The abstract concepts, prohibitions and demands of Calvinistic Christianity were difficult to understand and practice. But, after observing the good works and unselfishness of the majority of dedicated missionaries, the Hawaiians finally chose to accept the new religion.

The missionaries who came to Hawaii in the earliest years were of a special breed. The majority came from puritan New England, which explains much about their character. Naturally, the missionaries varied greatly in individual temperament, character, talent and training. As a group, they were far superior to the motley mixture of tradesmen, adventurers and riffraff flooding into the islands.

Judged by today's standards, many missionary ideas were extremely narrow and intolerant, for the churchmen were apt to see evil in the most innocent acts and scenes. But they did do many beneficial things for Hawaii. They reduced the Hawaiian language to written form, enabling the Hawaiian people to read and write in their own language. A mission press brought forth a considerable body of Hawaiian literature, text books, bibles, reviews, and even a Hawaiian-language newspaper.

Schools were established throughout the islands as rapidly as possible. The motivation was to instill religious ideas, but before long the mission schools were teaching many subjects not connected with religion. By 1831, only 11 years after the missionaries' arrival, some 52,000 pupils had been enrolled.

The missions also encouraged the development of agriculture and manufacture with which to give Hawaii an economic base in trading with foreign nations. They introduced western medicine and undertook the Kingdom's first modern census.

One more thing must be credited to the missionaries, something that even their detractors admit. They helped Hawaii become and remain an independent nation at a time when Hawaii was ripe for colonization. With their efforts, Hawaii was recognized as a legitimate kingdom governed along modern constitutional lines understood and respected by foreigners as well as Hawaiian citizens. These proselytizers of Christianity were primarily interested in the salvation of souls as they saw that task. They were also encharged with being an agency of civilization and, in their opinion, one thing was not possible without the other.

It is true that some missionaries "came to do good and did well." But it is an even greater truth that most of them came only to do good, and did just that.

A road in the leper settlement on Molokai's Kalawao Peninsula. In the distance, the spectacularly beautiful north Molokai coast.

Young victim of leprosy.

Youngsters of Kalaupapa. The Hawaiian people were alarmingly susceptible to this disease, as they were to all diseases brought in from the outside world.

36

Father Damien

Archives, State of Hawaii

On June 13, 1992, Pope John Paul II officially approved the "real miracle" attributed to Damien's intercession (the 1895 overnight cure from the seven-month long, grave intestinal disease of Sister Simplicia, who had been prying for a cure through Damien's intercession). On June 4, 1995, Pope John Paul II beatified Father Damien in a pontifical Mass in Brussels, Belgium, in recognition of a life of extraordinary holiness and heroic virtue. Beatification is the next to last formal step in the canonization process.

Joseph de Veuster was born on January 3, 1840 in Tremeloo, Belgium to a family of grain-growing peasants. Always a religious youth, Joseph entered the Sacred Hearts Congregation at Louvain as a postulant in 1859. This was the first step which would take him along the road to immortality as Father Damien, benefactor of the lepers of Molokai.

In the 1860's, Hawaii was alarmed at the spread of leprosy, particularly among the native Hawaiian people. Medical opinion held that the only way to prevent further spread of the disease was to isolate the victims. The Hawaiian Legislature passed an "Act to Prevent the Spread of Leprosy," choosing lonely Kalawao, a peninsula on Molokai's north shore, as the place of resettlement. Kalawao was a sort of triangular natural prison surrounded on two sides by rough seas and, at its back, cut off from the rest of the island by steep cliffs. The government planned to furnish farm animals, medical care, and regular shipments of food and other supplies.

In 1866 the first boatload of patients was torn from their weeping relatives and departed from Honolulu enroute to Kalawao. Upon arrival, they found that the so-called hospital had no beds, that medicines and doctors were in short supply, and that food shipments were undependable. Living in sordid conditions and cast out from society, most of the victims gave in to depression, hopelessness and alienation. Soon, the worst elements were running the settlement with the rest subject to their whims. No attempt whatsoever was made to cure the dread disease.

After completion of his training at Louvain, young Father Damien was assigned to the Sacred Hearts Mission in Hawaii and was ordained a priest in the Cathedral of Our Lady of Peace in Honolulu on May 21, 1864. On a visit with his Bishop (Maigret) to the leper settlement, Father Damien was struck with the suffering and almost total abandonment of the victims. He remained behind and soon asked the Bishop's permission that he be allowed to stay and serve the lepers. He had decided to dedicate his life to the alleviation of their physical and spiritual misery. Maigret responded by allowing him to remain as long as his devotion continued.

Father Damien's kindly, open nature would not permit anything to come between himself and his beloved charges. He worked alongside them, helped them to obtain better food and warm clothing, to build adequate housing, and to assure a supply of clean potable water. He built chapels and orphanages — his energy seemingly boundless. His enthusiastic and loving closeness to these unfortunates exacted its toll and he contracted leprosy. He continued to work as if nothing had happened. Eventually his selfless labors were recognized and the government undertook the responsibilities it had so long avoided.

As the news of his dedication and his work spread throughout the world, funds and help came pouring in. Father Damien worked as long as he was physically able. The Belgian peasant-priest died on April 15, 1889. Fellow lepers buried him under the tree where he had spent his first nights in the settlement. In 1936, at the request of the Belgian government, his body was returned to the village of his birth.

Today, the tiny settlement of Kalaupapa on Kalawao boasts modern facilities and the remaining patients lead nearly normal lives. The affliction is controllable with drugs and no one is forced to remain at Kalaupapa. But long-time residents consider it home and prefer to stay.

Whaling

The whaling industry had an enormous impact on the economy of Hawaii and dealt a mortal blow to what remained of traditional culture. At the height of the era, hundreds of ships and thousands of seamen crowded the towns of Honolulu and Lahaina as they awaited the seasonal gatherings of their prey in Arctic or Equatorial grounds. The first American whalers moved into the Pacific off Chile in 1791, as whales were becoming more and more scarce in the Atlantic. By 1819 they arrived in Hawaii, and in 1844 a fleet of 490 whaling ships anchored in Honolulu or off Lahaina on Maui.

Huge mobs of seamen thronged the towns, spending money "like drunken sailors." Living conditions aboard their ships were brutal, and long dull voyages with no respite ashore left them desperate for good times and excitement. In the Hawaiian ports they found women, alcohol, and plenty of brawls and trouble. A whaling sailor's idea of fun was diametrically opposed to the standards imposed by missionaries and the local establishment. The result was an almost constant clash with the authorities, all of which imparted a rather lively air to the dockside streets.

It was a case of "you can't live with 'em and you can't live without 'em." Tradesmen and craftsmen of all kinds, from blacksmiths, sundries merchants and carpenters, to the owners of grog shops and brothels, welcomed the economic stimulus provided by the whaling fleets while "decent folk" deplored the concurrent scandalous behavior.

Unlike today, with its highly mechanized system of pursuing the ever rarer whales with harpoon cannons and other refinements, the whaling industry of those days required brave men with strong backs. When a whale was sighted, they lowered small whaleboats and chased their prey. On closing with the leviathan, the harpooneer would plunge his weapon into the immense body at close range. Many crews were drowned or smashed to death in the ensuing struggle. In the drawing, Hulsart has depicted such a scene as it took place off one of the Hawaiian Islands, probably Maui.

Archives, State of Hawaii

It took boldness and strength to be a whaleman in those days and many lost their lives when the giant sea mammals smashed the tiny boats of their persecutors. Today the great whales are on the verge of extinction although various organizations are attempting to save them. The waters between Maui, Molokai and Lanai are winter calving grounds for hundreds of whales. Legislation is being sought to grant them sanctuary, thereby declaring this area a National Wildlife Refuge for these marine mammals.

Hawaiian Ways

By the end of the nineteenth century, the Hawaiians had experienced over one hundred years of contact with western technology and lifestyle, both of which stood in sharp contrast to their traditional ways. The resulting clash of ideals and values had a disastrous effect on the Hawaiian culture which was almost swept away amid a flood of new customs, beliefs and techniques.

First to succumb was the entire span of tools, weapons and utensils that had served so well through the long ages of Hawaii's pre-Western contact history. Next to suffer was the Hawaiian religion, rich in myth and ceremony, whose "kapu" system reflected a wise understanding that the land, the sea, and their natural products must not be wastefully exploited or abused. But the old religious beliefs could not be completely adhered to so long as Western intruders could violate the most sacred prohibitions of the gods without fear of punishment. In an action, perhaps without precedent anywhere on earth, Kamehameha II abolished Hawaii's religion in 1819, although some elements of the old religion survived with suprising strength, particularly the devotion to Pele, the volcano goddess.

With the loss of most of the stabilizing control of the old religion and the overwhelming impact of a new technology, the Hawaiian culture began a precipitous slide that seemed headed toward total extinction. Yet the ancient traditions and philosophy were not as fragile as it first appeared. People clung tenaciously to much of the best and strongest of their traditions, sensing the rightness of their beliefs and secure in the knowledge that they had much to teach and pass on to the newcomers who increasingly dominated their islands. Love and respect for the land, the idea that all people were of one family, the belief that all problems could be settled by honest and loving discourse — all this and more was like a great tree which could not be uprooted.

By the late 1800's, when some of the accompanying photographs were taken, many surface aspects of the old Hawaiian way of life were evident, particularly in remote country districts. Fishermen still plied the bays in outrigger canoes and speared their prey at night by torchlight. Whole villages turned out to pull in the giant "hukilau" fishnets and to share the catch as they had done since time immemorial. All the traditional foods were as popular as ever and still cooked in the Hawaiian "imu" or earth oven, and eaten at old-style "luau" feasts complete with songs and hulas of an earlier time. A few Hawaiians were even living in traditional houses thatched with pili grass. These were the outward remnants of the torn fabric that remained of the traditional life.

More importantly, much of the ancient spiritual undercurrent ran deep and strong despite more than a century of life in a society increasingly at odds with the basic Hawaiian attitude toward land, nature and humanity. The Polynesian attitude toward child-raising, the "hanai" system, was still prevalent. Children were often passed on to relatives or friends who had no children of their own. Hawaiian children grew up in a warm and affectionate world where people not related by blood were considered part of the "ohana" or extended family. To Hawaiians, the family not only consisted of the usual relatives, but included all who were loved or who chose to associate themselves in cooperative actions. Thus, when it seemed to outsiders that a Hawaiian had an unusually large number of relatives, it was only because of unfamiliarity with the Hawaiian concept of family. Another feature of the Hawaiian concept of family was a universal and unusual respect for elders.

Another old custom, widely practiced even today, was "ho'oponopono," a harmonious working out of conflict through frank discussions designed to set things right, to restore and maintain good relationships within the family or village group. It included prayer, respect for all viewpoints and, most significantly, the capacity for forgiveness. Hawaiians were not a competitive people. Their greatest strength lay in cooperation through the family or group. This lack of competitive spirit often put them at a disadvantage when dealing with people raised in a more ruthless and individualistic tradition.

Overall the Hawaiians felt that life should be happy and enjoyable. It was not necessary to be materially successful. Success was judged more on the basis of how well one was loved and by decency of character. Such attitudes were easier to maintain in the small rural villages than amid the anonymity and alienation of Honolulu.

Generosity was another feature of the old culture. Unfortunately this generousity was often interpreted as weakness or stupidity by those all too eager to take advantage. It is to their eternal credit that despite abuse, the Hawaiians in general are still known as a people of a loving and generous nature.

Hawaiian grass houses survived as late as the turn of the century. Here the basic design has been altered to include windows and a high entrance door.

Bishop M

Baker Photo, Robert E. Van Dyke Collection

An elderly Hawaiian man, rich in memories of the days when kings and chiefs ruled his independent Polynesian nation.

Baker Photo, Robert E. Van Dyke Collection

The coconut tree provided the Hawaiians with material for many uses. Among other things, its leaves were excellent for weaving light and attractive hats.

Baker Photo, Robert E. Van Dyke Collection

Hawaiian woman weaves a mat from the cured leaves of the hala (pandanus) tree. Hala provided a flexible durable and attractive material for handcrafting of many useful items.

Baker Photo, Robert E. Van Dyke Collection

A Hawaiian woman washes her clothes on the bank of a rapid stream.

An elderly couple repairing their fish net. A necessary but time-consuming task, it was nevertheless well suited to people whose concept of time was relaxed and unhurried.

Hawaiian man making poi. He is using all the traditional implements including poi-pounders, a pounding board, and poi and water containers made of calabash.

Hawaiian Ways

Many ancient Hawaiian customs still survive. This group has participated in a "hukilau" hauling in of a long fishnet. The catch was shared by all, though in this case the results are meager.

Right: Hawaiian fishermen in 1936 wear the traditional "malo" loin-cloth worn by Hawaiian men in the old days.

A Hawaiian man casting his net.

This memorable photograph was taken at a luau held at the Henry Poor residence in Waikiki in February 1889. At center is King David Kalakaua. On his right are Princess Liliuokalani (later Queen) and writer Robert Louis Stevenson. Seated at the king's left is Mrs. Thomas Stevenson, mother of the famed writer. The luau was an important feature of Hawaiian culture. It symbolized welcome and hospitality for the visitor. With everyone seated on the floor or the ground, it was certainly an easy way to put all at ease in getting to know each other. Despite the presence of even a king, a luau is, by its very nature, a relaxed and informal setting where enjoyment of food and good conversation take precedence.

44

Hawaiian Ways

The old and the new generation.

Camera Hawaii

Baker Photo, Robert E. Van Dyke Collection

The graceful charm of two old venerable Hawaiian ladies.

City Hawaiians demonstrate techniques for eating poi.

Robert E. Van Dyke Collection

Hawaiian Ways

Queen Liliuokalani loved country life away from palace intrigue. Here she could relax and, for a while, forget the cares of state and the formal life her position imposed upon her. Photographs taken in those days tend to appear posed: picture taking was still an uncommon experience for most people and the longer exposure time required that people sit very still. Queen Liliuokalani is seated third from the left in this group.

Baker Photo, Robert E. Van Dyke Collection

Photographer Baker delighted in capturing the children of Hawaii at play. Town life at the turn of the century was a bit prudish but Hawaiian country children were blissfully unaware as they played by the sea, their bodies healthfully exposed to sun, water and fresh air.

Right: This little girl of mixed Hawaiian-Japanese ancestry was photographed on the island of Molokai in 1912. To this day Molokai remains a stronghold of the Hawaiian way of life, a place where time flows at a leisurely pace.

Hawaiian girl.   Baker Photo, Robert E. Van Dyke Collection

Baker Photo, Robert E. Van Dyke Collection

IN GRATITUDE

It is impossible to do any photographic research about Hawaii without feeling respect and gratitude for the work of Ray Jerome Baker who some called the "Matthew Brady of Hawaii." He arrived in Hawaii in 1910 to begin a work that can rightfully be described as prodigious. Baker took photographs of every nook and cranny of Honolulu, recording for posterity what street corners, buildings and houses looked like at the time. In addition to his own voluminous record Baker bought up old photographs of Hawaii taken by photographers of the nineteenth century. His photographs of the Hawaiian people preserve a natural vision of a way of life that has now disappeared. He was an innovative photographer and, in private life, an unorthodox and fearless defender of often unpopular causes. He died in Honolulu on October 27, 1972, aged ninety-one.

Hawaiian Ways

Ever since Western man entered the Pacific Ocean, sailors and other travelers brought back fascinating accounts of amorous and beautiful Polynesian women. This legend was one borne out by facts. Polynesian women were, and are, often strikingly beautiful. The five Hawaiian girls in this photo, taken in 1890, are typically Polynesian in appearance, with little to distinguish them from their sisters in Tahiti, Samoa or Tonga. Only the "Mother Hubbard" dresses they wear tell of one hundred years of Western influence.

Baker Collection, Bishop Museum

The attractive young miss of Chinese and Hawaiian ancestry in this old photo typifies the beauty resulting from Hawaii's complicated blending of diverse peoples.

Robert E. Van Dyke Collection

This Hawaiian girl swimmer wears what might be a forerunner of today's popular T-shirts with their humorous and advertising messages. In this case, the Hilo Tribune has stamped its logo on one of those scratchy wool swim suits worn in 1926 when this photo was taken.

Left: Portrait of a Hawaiian cowboy. They are called "paniolo" which is a Hawaiian language version of the word "Espanol." This is due to the fact that Hawaii's first cowboys were Spanish-speaking cowboys brought in from Mexico for their skill at ranching tasks. Hawaiian's took to cattle ranching with great enthusiasm but the old name, "paniolo" continues to this day.

Rick Golt

Robert E. Van Dyke Col

Pa'u riders in Kapiolani Park, June 11, 1900. The word "Pa'u" refers to the voluminous wraparound skirts worn by women riders both as a protection for their clothing like a cowboy's chaps and also for decorative effect. The pa'u was originally the tapa cloth garment worn by Hawaiian women in pre-western-contact times.

The imposing presence and dignity of old Hawaii's alii class are captured in this portrait taken near the turn of the century.

This Hawaiian girl at the turn of the century combines stylishness and fashion with delightful touches derived from the customs of her ancestors.

Hawaiian Ways

The melancholy of a disappearing people emanates from these sweet, sad faces. Yet, the pensive mood will pass as they sing lively Hawaiian songs to the strum of their guitar.

Hula

Despite efforts of missionaries and other bluenoses among the non-Hawaiian population, the hula never became extinct although it faded from public sight during the middle decades of the nineteenth century. For a long time this authentic native dance form existed underground, banished from the towns but still quietly and surreptitiously performed among the rural people.

At one time there were some 300 distinct hulas in the Hawaiian repertoire. When Westerners arrived in Hawaii, the hula was Hawaii's living theater, danced as an accompaniment to poetry. It was also a form of religious rite to honor the gods and the chiefs. It was usually dedicated to its patroness Laka, goddess of the hula.

The ancient Hawaiian dances were performed by both men and women, though not usually at the same time. The men's hulas were vigorous and forceful while those of the women were more sensual and esthetic. The sacred hulas were delicate, artistic and subtle forms of dance, mastered only after long years of apprenticeship under a master teacher. Today, a rare few masters of this ancient art form carry on the tradition.

Beside the solemn sacred hula, there always existed a more "profane" form, to entertain and gladden the hearts of both the alii class and the common people. Most of today's dances are descended from this popular type of hula.

Early missionaries disliked the hula they saw. The sight of scantily clad women moving in rhythm to poetry offended their puritan ethics, and they made strenuous efforts to abolish this aspect of ancient Hawaiian culture once their authority was established.

Several of Hawaii's monarchs recognized that the extinction of the hula would mean the end of an important cultural aspect of the severely battered Hawaiian civilization. Hawaiians were already demoralized by the destruction Western ways had wreaked on their way of life. These Hawaiian kings encouraged the revival of the hula despite missionary objections.

King David Kalakaua was particularly enthusiastic about reviving the hula in all its splendor and joy. During his reign professional hula troupes became popular again and they meandered about entertaining people at luaus, public occasions and the theater. Accompanying photos show some of these troupes. One in particular is remarkable for its time (circa 1900) because of the natural pride with which the girls expose their breasts in the unashamed ways of their ancestors.

For a time, the lovely hulas of Hawaii were in danger of disappearing forever. Thanks to the foresight and wisdom of Hawaii's kings, Hawaii's unique and graceful national dances are still seen today and are more popular than ever.

Archives, State of Hawaii

Hula

Many of the original sketches made by early European artists who came to Hawaii with various exploring expeditions were later retouched by copyists who changed the body and facial appearance of the Hawaiians to conform to the continental idea of beauty. But in this engraving by Choris, the Hawaiian male dancers appear more nearly true to their actual appearance. The dancers are carrying elaborately decorated feather-embellished gourd rattles. On their legs they wear anklets consisting of hundreds of dog teeth which made distinctive rattling sounds to accompany their leg movements. The man in the center is heavily tattooed from forehead to waist. Such tattooing was widespread in ancient Polynesia, and the Hawaiians developed very specialized designs. Bracelets of large boar tusks decorate their wrists and doubtlesly contributed visual impact to the arm movements, so important in Hawaiian dancing. The dancers are not wearing the customery "malo" (men's loin cloth) but seem to be wearing intricately wrapped tapa cloth or even imported cotton cloth from a trading ship. In the background, the musicians rhythmically accompany the dancers with gourd drums and by tapping on coconut shells with a short stick. Such dancing was often combined with the singing of poetic chants or "mele" which usually told a story while the dance depicted the actions or concepts of the story. The Hawaiian dance, or hula, was performed by both men and women. The men's hulas were vigorous and forceful while those of the women were more sensual or esthetic. Today's hulas are only a remnant of what was once a very complex and sacred repertoire, though the renewed consciousness of Hawaii's heritage is restoring much of the ancient vigor and variety. Men's hulas, once fallen virtually into disuse, are staging a strong comeback and add virility to hula demonstrations that up until recently were almost exclusively the province of women.

Hula

In this engraving the musicians are less visible than in that of the male dancers, but gourd drums and chanting provided the basic accompaniment. Other Hawaiian musical instruments included bamboo nose flutes, wooden drums with sharkskin heads, feather decorated gourd rattles, smooth stones which were clicked together to make a castanet-like sound, bamboo rattles and hula sticks for beating time. They also used small gourd whistles, which were unique to Hawaii. Shell trumpets made a very distinctive and mournful sound which could literally be heard for miles. These conch shell trumpets were extensively used on occasions of high ceremony. The women's hair, in this illustration, has been whitened above the forehead by application of a lime paste made of crushed coral, a practice that even today is widespread in southern Polynesia and Melanesia. The short hair shown on the women does not fit our standard image of the legendary south seas maiden with raven locks to her knees, but was nevertheless not at all uncommon in many island groups. In the more remote islands of southern Polynesia, married women are often recognized by their shorn hair. Dancing skirts varied widely. In this portrait, the dancers appear to be wearing tapa cloth wraparounds with complicated knots and bows. The "grass" skirt used often in nightclub and movie presentations is not authentically Hawaiian. This particular costume was introduced to Hawaii by Gilbert Islanders many decades after the scene depicted above.

In this photo taken in the 1870's the girls wear long dresses covered by tapa cloth wrap-around skirts. Despite suppression, the hula has survived. Many ancient hulas are forgotten and there have been inevitable changes in style, but the Hawaiian national dance is as Polynesian as ever.

These uninhibited young women pose in the natural manner of their ancestors. Considering the general western outlook of the 80's, the photo is a bold one for its time.

Beginning in Kalakaua's reign, hula troupes became very popular and many performed at theaters as well as luaus. The women in this hula troupe are quite serious as they pose for the photographer in the late 1890's. The clothing shows the influence of 100 years of western contact.

Hula

George Mellen, Robert E. Van Dyke Collection

Despite the fact that the thirties were a low point in the appreciation of Hawaii's native cultural arts, the hula was still going strong as shown by these graceful and enthusiastic youngsters in 1936.

George Mellen, Robert E. Van Dyke Collection

Ah for the good old days! This nostalgic photo was taken in 1937 by George Mellen of young dancer Annie Nihipali accompanied by Charles on the ukulele and Herbert on the guitar.

Sweet Agriculture

Sugar cane was one of the food plants brought along to Hawaii by the Polynesian settlers in their great canoe voyages from southern Polynesia. In the journal of his voyage to Hawaii, Captain Cook mentioned seeing sugar cane in Hawaiian gardens.

There were sporadic attempts at commercial sugar-cane growing and the manufacture of sugar in the early 1800's. Boki, the Governor of Oahu, entered a partnership with English agriculturist John Wilkinson in 1825 and established a plantation in Honolulu's Manoa Valley. The first continuing sugar plantation was begun by Ladd & Co., on Kauai in 1835.

Up until the late 1840's and the early 1850's there was no imperative for expansion of the tiny sugar industry, although the early missionaries recognized the need to expand and diversify Hawaii's economy which depended heavily on the visits of the huge whaling fleets. The California Gold Rush in 1849 provided a temporary stimulus since Hawaii's sugar found a ready market that paid high prices. But by 1851 the gold rush was over and the lucrative West Coast market collapsed. However, by the end of the 1850's, the West Coast market was recovering as California and Oregon grew in population. The number of sugar-cane plantations began to grow as sugar prices went on the upswing.

The American Civil War proved to be a bonanza for the Hawaiian sugar industry. Prices zoomed so high that Hawaiian planters could make a profit despite the high entry tariff paid at American ports. By 1866, Hawaii was exporting almost eighteen million pounds of sugar compared to a mere one-and-a-half million pounds only six years earlier. The real boon to the sugar industry was to come with the reciprocity treaty of 1876, which eliminated the heavy tariff on Hawaiian sugar entering U.S. ports.

As the sugar industry grew, it became apparent that a severe labor shortage was developing. Native Hawaiian people were declining in numbers due to disease and a low birth rate. They already contributed a high percentage of their men to the plantation labor force. The solution decided upon was to import foreign contract labor, both as a means of combatting the labor shortage and bolstering the declining island population. Where possible, the Hawaiian authorities looked to recruit peoples with some sort of racial affinity to the native Hawaiian people, but the majority of these recruits were to come from the Philippines, Japan, Korea and China. The few Gilbert Islanders brought in from Micronesia were overcome by homesickness and proved most unsatisfactory.

Life on the plantation, at least in the early days, was hard and many contract workers left the plantations once their contracts had expired. Refusal to work could be punished by imprisonment at hard labor until the offender consented to return to his job. There were, of course, provisions to protect the contract laborer from many forms of abuse. Whatever its drawbacks, the contract labor system brought new people to Hawaii, people who eventually became a stable body of American citizens. Their descendants would become Hawaii's future leaders.

The sugar industry constantly sought to improve its methods and the purity of its raw sugar, experimenting with new varieties of cane, new equipment and techniques of growing, harvesting and milling. Tunnels were dug through mountains, trestles and ditches were made to span valleys to carry water to irrigate dry but fertile lands. This allowed an enormous expansion of the acreage devoted to sugar cane. Former wastelands became green and productive, and Hawaii gained a steady and dependable income from this vital agricultural industry.

Sweet Agriculture

Plantation towns were lonely, isolated in the midst of vast sugar cane fields far removed from the towns and cities. The homes of the workers were dominated by the mill structures. Shown here is remote Hana Plantation on the eastern shore of Maui at the turn of the century.

Many Hawaii residents today can recall a childhood spent in a plantation home similar to the one in this photograph. Housing for plantation labor was set up in small village-like groups of homes and barracks called camps. Often the inhabitants were of a single ethnic group and the tiny villages came to be known as "Portuguese Camp" or "Filipino Camp," as the case may have been. Some of these houses may still be seen in the country districts.

Recently arrived from Spain, these plantation workers pose in front of their Lahaina home in 1915.

Sweet Agriculture
Claus Spreckels - Titan of Hawaiian Sugar

A San Francisco sugar refiner with an eye for the main chance, Spreckels cornered the 1877 Hawaiian sugar crop and rose to a position of power in the affairs of the kingdom. As an advisor to King Kalakaua, he helped promote many dubious financial and political schemes. He purchased his power by bank rolling the freespending King's pet projects at high rates of interest. The end result was that Kalakaua found himself almost totally indebted to Spreckels. Allowing arrogance to cloud his good judgement, the normally shrewd Spreckels lost favor with the King through displays of dictatorial behavior. Finally he was bought off and left the islands. A ruthless and unscrupulous business man, he nevertheless contributed greatly to the expansion of the Hawaiian sugar industry

Baker Photo, Robert E. Van Dyke Collection

The Spreckels mansion on Punahou Street photographed in 1908. Sumptuous and baronial, it was built at a cost of $100,000 in an age when the dollar was worth many times its present value. During the height of Spreckels' power, this Victorian palace was the scene of lavish dinner parties and dances.

Baker Photo, Robert E. Van Dyke Collection

Claus Spreckels, refiner, planter, and "king" of Hawaiian sugar. He gained undue influence in Kalakaua's government by allowing the King to become heavily indebted to him.

Pineapple

Golden Fruit of Hawaii

The word pineapple almost automatically evokes an association with Hawaii. It was in Hawaii that the growing of pineapples first became a big business, and today the Hawaiian pineapple, despite increasing competition from other areas, is among the most delicious produced anywhere.

While the Hawaiians brought many plants with them from their homelands, the pineapple was not one of them. The Hawaiians called the pineapple "hala kahiki" meaning "the foreign pandanus," because of its superficial resemblance to the fruit of the pandanus trees.

Commercial pineapple planting in Hawaii got off to a rather hesitant start about the middle of the nineteenth century at Kailua-Kona on the island of Hawaii. A variety known as the "Wild Kailua" was traded to whaling ships and many tons were sent to the growing towns and settlements in California. Due to a high spoilage rate, the business failed.

In 1886, an Englishman, John Kidwell, brought in a variety known as the "Smooth Cayenne." Because of its uniform size and delicious flavor, it is still the standard variety grown today. Since the fruit was too perishable to withstand the long journey to the West Coast in those days, Kidwell realized that the only practical way to enter the American market would be to can the fruit. Though his venture failed, he had the right idea.

In 1899, James D. Dole arrived in Hawaii. With borrowed capital he established large plantations in central Oahu near Wahiawa and then built a cannery right next to the fields. In 1903, the first pack of canned pineapple was produced—about 1,800 cases. Today, the same amount is packed in minutes.

The pineapple industry has been diminishing in importance because of sharply increased production costs and competition from pineapples produced in other areas by cheaper labor. However, pineapple's prospects are now improving with the development of a mainland market for air-flown fresh pineapple. This golden crop still remains a vital part of Hawaii's economy. Pineapple fields provide broad open spaces amid urban encroachment and help preserve Hawaii's scenery.

Hawaiian Pineapp

James Drummond Dole plowing his first pineapple field in 1901 near Wahiawa. Dole is on the right. This field was the beginning of the immense pineapple plantations that cover much of Oahu's central plateau. Others in the photo include Fred Tracy, and Inez and Muriel Gibson.

Newcomers

The Hawaiians had been in these islands for at least a thousand years when a new group of people burst through the encircling horizon, the first of many racial and national groups that would come to settle and eventually call Hawaii their home. The first newcomers were people of European ancestry, beginning with the English under Captain Cook and then Americans who came as explorers, adventurers, businessmen and missionaries.

At first, all foreigners were known as "haole," which means outsiders or non-Hawaiians. Since the first foreigners that the Hawaiians saw were Europeans, the word soon came to refer strictly to persons of European ancestry. This meaning continues to this day although sometimes it can also be used derogatorily.

For many decades after Hawaii's initial contact with the outside world, the number of Caucasian residents in the islands was very small. The early whites were missionaries, tradesman, whaling and merchant seamen and assorted others. Later, some whites were brought in as plantation laborers but, except for the Portuguese, they never formed a significant part of the plantation labor force.

Among the Caucasians who came in small groups as agricultural workers were Russians, Portuguese, Spaniards, Germans and Norwegians. Since many of them, along with whites of American and British ancestry, intermarried with Hawaiians and other racial groups, it became difficult for census-takers to fit people into neat classifications as to who was Caucasian and who was not.

The 1853 census showed a white resident population of only 1,887. But, throughout this early period whites held influence and power far out of proportion to their numbers, a fact which led to considerable resentment. Many rose high in positions of trust as advisors to the Hawaiian monarchy. Others formed the core of the business establishment and held virtually uncontested economic power. Of course, not all Caucasians held great economic or political power. Many were people of modest means — professionals, tradesmen, clerks and other everyday occupations. A few were paupers and derelicts, but certainly most were at least comfortably well off compared to the rest of the population.

Newcomers of European ancestry were only the first in a series of population waves bringing in people from many countries who would eventually far outnumber the native Hawaiian population. Next to come in large numbers were the Chinese, then the Japanese, Portuguese, Filipinos, Koreans, Puerto Ricans, Samoans, as well as a liberal sprinkling of people from other parts of the world. And, once here, they seldom kept exclusively to themselves, but mixed together in a potpourri of some of the most interesting racial mixtures to be found anywhere.

Hawaii's multi-racial nature started with the arrival of Cook's expedition and continues to this day. The Hawaiians usually welcomed strangers, and the welcome could be warm indeed. The uninhibited and generous-natured Hawaiians set no racial barriers in choosing partners.

Within two generations of contact with the western world, a mixed community had sprung up, and many of Hawaii's oldest and most distinguished families are of such ancestry. At first, the combinations were predominantly Polynesian-European. The offspring of these marriages often resulted in beautiful and vivacious children.

Later, as the Chinese, Japanese, Filipinos, Portuguese and many others arrived, the blendings became progressively more complicated and cosmopolitan. The beauty of the women and the handsomeness of the men seemed to grow in direct proportion to the complexity of their genetic heritage.

The trend continues. Nearly forty percent of all marriages in the state of Hawaii are interracial. People of cosmopolitan ancestry, particularly part-Hawaiian, make up about one-fourth of the state's population. Census analysis reveals that Hawaii's resident population today can be broken down as follows: 21.5 percent Caucasian (not a great deal higher than the 18 percent of 1900), 30.2 percent Japanese, 18.2 percent part-Hawaiian, 10.8 percent Filipino, 9.4 percent mixed non-Hawaiian, 4.9 percent Chinese, 1.4 percent Korean, 0.5 percent Samoan, 0.3 percent Puerto Rican, 0.2 percent Afro-American. Sad to say, today only 1.5 percent of the State's population is of pure Hawaiian ancestry.

By the 1880's, when this photo was taken, Chinese laborers were arriving yearly by the thousands in Honolulu to be transhipped to plantations on the Outer Islands.

Stores like this had social as well as economic value for Hawaii's Chinese population. They served mostly as clubs where a man could write to or receive letters from his home village in China. The owner usually lived upstairs and a new immigrant or an out-of-town visitor could enjoy a meal or spend the night. During the period from 1877 to 1889, over fifty-percent of Hawaii's retail stores were Chinese-owned or operated.

Newcomers

The Chinese

The first major group of indentured Chinese plantation workers arrived in 1852, although an individual Chinese was observed in 1794 in the retinue of King Kamehameha I at Kealakekua Bay, and it was rumored that a Chinese man living on Lanai milled and boiled sugar in 1802.

Between 1852 and 1856, several thousand Chinese "coolies" were brought in to labor on the plantations. The census of 1878 counted 6,045 as the Chinese population of the islands. By 1884, this number had risen to 18,254. The Chinese laborers were industrious and well-behaved although they were quick to resent injustices. They were also intelligent and ambitious. As soon as their indentured-labor contracts were fulfilled, most of them headed straight for Honolulu and other towns to enter trade and open their own small businesses.

The Chinese people who migrated to Hawaii were mostly Cantonese from the Pearl River Delta near Macao. Another major dialect group among the immigrants were the Hakka who came from areas closer to Hong Kong. Because many Chinese dialects are mutually unintelligible, communication between two groups of Chinese was often difficult. An observer in the year 1856 was amused to see two groups of Chinese who spoke differing dialects communicating with each other quite adequately by using the Hawaiian language, which they had learned while working on the plantations.

The Chinese laborers soon came to be considered a problem in Hawaii because of their growing numbers and the fact that they were mostly male. Quite a few Chinese married Hawaiian women. As a result, Hawaiian-Chinese families are common in Hawaii today. Another reason for resentment was that the Chinese proved to be astute and hard-working businessmen, offering competition to the other tradesmen. Before the end of the nineteenth century there were many rich Chinese families in Honolulu. The growing Chinese population which so worried Hawaii in the late 1880's was soon to be outnumbered by the even larger Japanese immigration.

Baker Collection, Bishop Museum

This cheerful soul hawked his tasty "manapua" in the Ewa district of Oahu about 1915. Manapua is a bread dumpling with a meatfilled center. He and others like him were once a common sight in Honolulu. Alas, "progress" has taken its toll and few remain to contribute a picturesque note to daily life in the islands.

Newcomers

The Japanese

This photo shows, in microcosm, the assimilation of Hawaii's immigrant groups. Originally recruited as contract labor for the sugar and pineapple plantations, one group after another, the Chinese, the Portuguese, the Japanese, the Filipinos, followed almost the same steps toward entry into the mainstream of island life and Americanization. The oldest generation, once their plantation contracts were fulfilled, became small shop owners and tradesmen, sacrificing themselves on meager incomes to assure that their children would do better. The next generation, with the advantages of education unavailable to their parents, entered the professional and white-collar jobs. The gradually evolving lifestyles accompanying this change are reflected in the clothing worn when this photo was taken in 1928. It ranges from the somber, conservative garb of the older men and the old-country kimonos of the women to the American schoolday dress of the children. Any doubt about the importance of Americans of Japanese ancestry was dispelled with the election of George Ariyoshi as Governor of Hawaii in 1974. He was elected by all the people of Hawaii and did not depend solely on the Japanese-American vote. With complete impartiality, many Americans of Japanese ancestry voted for his opponents both in the primary and general elections.

Newcomers

The Japanese

Newly arrived Japanese agricultural workers with plantation housing in background.

Archives, State of Hawaii

Hawaii saw its first Japanese contract workers in 1868 when a small group of 148 were recruited, against the wishes of the Japanese government. It was not until 1886, when an agreement was signed between the governments of Hawaii and Japan, that Japanese immigrants began to arrive in large numbers.

In 1890 there were 12,610 Japanese listed in the census and the figure grew to 61,111 by 1900. Unlike the other countries from which contract workers originated, Japan carefully monitored how her sons were being treated in the islands and regularly sent inspection teams to the plantations to take note of grievances. Japan also set up offices in Honolulu to facilitate the recruiting process and to oversee the welfare of those recruited.

By the early 1900's, Japanese made up some 40 percent of the population of the islands. As the male laborers sent for wives and children as well as mail-order brides, the Japanese population grew and hostility toward them mounted. One outgrowth of this hostility was the passage of the Federal Exclusion Act in 1924 which almost completely halted any further immigration from Japan.

Newcomers

The Portuguese

The majority of plantation laborers recruited to Hawaii came from the Far East. However, some also emigrated from Europe. Of these, the Portuguese formed the largest contingent. Actually, very few came from Portugal itself, but were from the Atlantic islands of Madeira and the Azores.

Most of the 17,500 Portuguese contract workers recruited for Hawaii's plantations arrived between 1878 and 1887. The Hawaiian census counted 486 Portuguese in the islands in 1878. By 1884, that number had risen to 9,967.

Like other plantation workers before them, the Portuguese were eager to leave the plantations once their contracts had expired. Some planters were not too happy with the Portuguese, who demanded higher salaries than the Orientals, were less submissive and had recourse to the Portuguese Consulate. Though many Portuguese women and children accompanied their men to Hawaii, intermarriage with Hawaiians was not uncommon. Today there are many persons of mixed Portuguese-Hawaiian ancestry.

Some Portuguese plantation workers who left work on sugar plantations set themselves up in business or bought plots of land for truck gardening.

Multi-Cultural

Above Right: This tiny Portuguese-owned store beside a remote country road sold staple supplies to plantation workers from nearby camps.

Lower Right: Portuguese women baking bread— 1908. The Portuguese cling to many of their national customs here in the islands. These Portuguese women are baking "pao doce" (sweet bread) in a backyard oven.

Bishop M

Newcomers

The Portuguese

Above: Portuguese women plantation workers from the Atlantic islands of Madeira and the Azores wearing the picturesque hats of their distant homeland. Many Portuguese customs have survived in the new Hawaiian homeland, particularly as concerns food. Today, everyone in the islands enjoys "malasadas," a kind of fluffy doughnut without a hole, served hot and sprinkled with sugar. Portuguese bean soup is another highly appreciated item on island restaurant menus.

Right: A Portuguese family get-together in Lahaina, Maui, about 1915. The Portuguese originally tended to settle together in local communities. One such, on the slopes of Honolulu's Punchbowl crater, is still a predominantly Portuguese area, and many others remain throughout the islands.

Newcomers

The Koreans

A few small groups of Korean merchants were present in Hawaii as early as 1899, but it was not until January 13, 1903, that the first major group of immigrants arrived. This was marked by the arrival of the S.S. Gaelic from Inchon, Korea, which carried 101 persons — fifty-five men, twenty-one women and twenty-five children.

At this time plantation owners in Hawaii were looking at Korea as a possible source of plantation labor. During the next two and a half years, sixty-five boatloads of Korean laborers landed in Honolulu with 7,843 passengers. Upon their arrival, the immigrants were scattered to plantations on Oahu and the Big Island.

In April, 1905, the Emperor of Korea decreed the stoppage of emigration from his country because of official Korean concern over rumored distresses suffered by Koreans who had emigrated to Mexico. This threw a cloud of suspicion over all labor emigration.

Between 1911 and 1924, many of the bachelor Korean immigrants sent home for "picture brides." Eight hundred Korean women arrived. Subsequently, the number of families increased and helped to stabilize the Korean population in Hawaii.

Most of the Koreans had no desire to remain on plantations. Some started boarding houses — couples took in single Korean men as roomers and the women cooked. Other Koreans turned successfully to food manufacturing, tailoring, carpentry, laundry and other trades.

A Korean family all dressed up for a visit to the photographer's studio. The husband has become Americanized in his clothing but the more tradition-minded wife clings to her native Korean style of dress.

Newcomers

The Filipinos

The Filipinos were the last large-scale arrival of immigrant groups recruited to Hawaii as plantation laborers. They were drawn mainly from various agricultural populations within the Philippine Islands — Tagalogs, Visayans, and Ilocanos. Between 1907 and 1931, nearly 120,000 Filipinos, mostly males, came to the islands.

The Filipinos brought many customs of their homeland. Their heritage combines that of their native islands with a rich overlay of Spanish influence resulting from almost 400 years as part of the Spanish empire. In Filipino dances, exotic costumes and rhythms of the Philippine Islands blend with the stateliness and fire of Spanish dances for a visually stunning effect. And the Filipina women of Hawaii must be included among the world's most beautiful.

As the last to arrive in Hawaii in large numbers, the Filipinos have not yet had full opportunity to move upward in the economic picture. Ironically, many highly trained Filipino professionals are working at jobs beneath their capacities due to difficulties in obtaining American accreditation or licenses for degrees and skills gained in their home country. Politically, their power has not yet made itself apparent and this may be due to the fact that Filipino immigrants have come from widely differing language areas and various levels of their home society, all of which tends to impede cooperation on the community level. Younger generations, more thoroughly integrated into Hawaiian society, will doubtless change this set of circumstances.

A Filipino worker's family awaits the father's return from his labors at the door of their tiny plantation-town house..

Newcomers

The Puerto Ricans

Much is made of Hawaii's rainbow mixture of peoples resulting from the intermarriage of people of diverse ethnic and racial backgrounds. However, one group that arrived in Hawaii already qualified as a racially mixed people were the Puerto Ricans. In their Caribbean island home, they had for centuries practiced a kind of racial harmony known in very few parts of the world. The basic ancestry of the Puerto Rican people consists of pre-Columbian Indians, Caucasians of Spanish origin, and blacks of African descent. After centuries of intermingling, many Puerto Rican families carried genes of all three groups in varying amounts.

On December 23, 1900, the ship *Rio de Janeiro* entered Honolulu harbor with the first significant group of Puerto Ricans brought to Hawaii for plantation work. In the years 1900 and 1901, some 5,200 more came to try their fortunes in Hawaii, prompted by severe hurricane destruction in their home island. About 2,400 were men who had signed up for a three year agricultural contract. The remainder were women and children.

Due to some similarities in culture and general appearance, the Puerto Ricans intermarried frequently with Filipinos, Portuguese, Spaniards and Hawaiians. Puerto Rican families per se grew rapidly since they were among the few immigrant groups that initially included women and children. The 1950 census, the last in Hawaii which counted Puerto Ricans as a separate group, gave a Puerto Rican population of 10,000.

To a great extent the Puerto Ricans have melded into the general population of Hawaii, not really considering themselves any longer a separate group. Nevertheless, many of the older people still speak Spanish and prepare the delicious food specialties of that Caribbean island, a cuisine that is quite similar to traditional Cuban fare. In line with recent trends among various ethnic groups, Hawaiians of Puerto Rican ancestry are showing a renewed interest in their cultural and ancestral background.

The Norma Carr Collection

Mary and Basilio Salcedo, brother and sister, born in Hawaii to parents who migrated from Puerto Rico. This portrait was taken in 1915.

Newcomers

The majority of the diverse peoples who came to Hawaii were originally

Either amused by the cameraman or sharing a private joke, these girls of Samoan ancestry find Hawaii a congenial place to live. Though often confused by a set of values differing from those of their South Seas homeland, Samoans are adapting to life in Hawaii-while at the same time preserving a proud sense of their own colorful heritage.

brought in as plantation labor and later moved out of the plantations to join Hawaii's mainstream. None of these peoples however were Polynesians, racially and culturally akin to the native Hawaiians. There were a few exceptions when Gilbertese and a few other Pacific Islanders were recruited for plantation work. But they were small in number and totally unsuited to the hard and monotonous labor. Eventually most of them returned to their home islands and no further recruitment of Pacific Islanders was sought.

The Samoan migration to Hawaii was unique in that the Samoans did not come as plantation workers and they were the only significant group of Polynesian migrants to Hawaii. Samoa consists of a group of islands about 3,000 miles slightly southwest of Hawaii. It is now believed that in the islands of Samoa and nearby Tonga, the Polynesians first became a racially and culturally distinct people, later voyaging forth to discover the vast skein of islands that today comprise what is known as Polynesia.

The first large group of Samoans came to Hawaii in 1919 when the Mormon temple was built in Laie on Oahu's northeastern shore. Mormonism had long taken root in Samoa. At Laie they formed a primarily agricultural group, which by 1950, numbered about 500 people.

In 1952 about 1,000 Samoans arrived in Hawaii. They were mostly naval personnel and their dependents transferred here due to the phasing out of the U.S. naval base on Tutuila, the main island of American Samoa. As American nationals, the Samoans were able to enter Hawaii without going through immigration procedures. It is estimated that there are presently more than 13,000 Samoans and part-Samoans resident in

Hawaii, the majority of them on Oahu.

To a great extent, Hawaii's Samoans have preserved their colorful ways and the Samoan language is in daily use in Samoan communities. The Samoans come from an area of Polynesia where the ancient traditions are still suprisingly intact despite centuries of contact with the western world. Strongly patriotic, with love and pride for their homeland and its culture, Samoans here and at home have long practiced a concept known in Samoa as "Fa'a Samoa" which means, "the Samoan Way." Through this concept, each generation is instilled with pride in the culture and language of Samoa. It is this that has helped preserve the old Samoan way of life.

Samoan culture has traditionally exalted cooperation and submission to chiefs and elders as opposed to individualism. To some extent, this lack of competitive spirit has been a hindrance to progress in today's western culture. While the chieftainship structure is still strong, it is meeting increasing resistance from youngsters more exposed than their parents to western ways. Samoan communal ideas of property have also caused conflict in a society where property is considered an individual rather than a group possession.

One of Oahu's most colorful events is held every year when the Samoan community celebrates Flag Day in memory of the time when American Samoa came under the American flag. It is on this day that all the bright colors, traditional dances and soaring a capella songs are sung amidst huge quantities of Samoan foods spread out for one and all. It is a day when Samoans from all walks of life lay aside their western clothes and put on lava-lavas, face paints, and symbols to relive once again the ancient times.

Old Honolulu

Archives, State of

Kawaiahao Church as seen in 1887 from the Judiciary Building. Such an unimpeded view toward Diamond Head is now a thing of the past. Oahu's oldest and most important Hawaiian church was constructed between 1836 and 1842 under the direction of missionary leader Hiram Bingham.

Old Honolulu

Old Honolulu grew up beside a harbor that once boasted only a tiny village of grass thatched houses on a dusty plain. The name of this village was Kou. By 1857, Honolulu ("protected harbor" in the Hawaiian language) had become one of the Pacific's major seaports, prospering on services of the whaling fleets and merchantmen plying between the West Coast and the Orient.

Honolulu's advantages as a port outstripped the attractions of other Hawaiian port towns. It offered the safest anchorage, the only shipyard, and the biggest town in the islands. And consequently, it soon sheltered the greatest number of ships. The resulting prosperity was reflected in the improving image of downtown Honolulu. There were mean and sordid streets in 1857, as indeed there are to the present day. But the general aspect of the city's business center became more pleasing to the eye. As wealth brought pride, Honolulu's affluent merchants and business establishments began to impose an orderliness and solidity previously unknown.

Robert E. Van Dyke Collection

The Honolulu residence of John A. Cummins, located at Pawaa, site of Washington School (originally called Cummins School) on King Street. The house was built in the summer of 1880. This photo, taken on February 21, 1901 shows Mrs. James Campbell and children; Matilda Walker and Kahai; Capt. John Ross standing in back; and J. A. Cummins to the left in a white beard. On April 17, 1901 Mrs. Campbell and children left for Europe on the Steamer Mariposa. Mrs. Campbell later married Col. Sam Parker, owner of Parker Ranch, and her daughter Abigail married Prince David Kawananakoa a few days later in San Francisco.

Old Honolulu

Junction of Union and Hotel Street, 1870

Merchant Street in horse and buggy days, lined with mercantile establishments large and small, 1880.

Archives, State of Hawaii

Old Honolulu

CITY FURNITURE STORE.
H.H. WILLIAMS, MANAGER.
UNDERTAKER & EMBALMER.
MEA I'ALOA. HANA PAHU
AME KAA KUPAPAU.
AMORTALHADOR E EMBALSAMADOR
EMPREZA FUNERARIA.

Archives, State of

Fort Street has certainly changed. The horse and buggy traffic had rough going when rains turned the street into a quagmire. At first, Honolulu's larger structures were built of bricks shipped to the Islands in sailing vessels, but later, Hawaiian lava rock was used more often, 1886.

The motor car brought traffic officers to Honolulu's major intersections in the days before electric traffic signals. The photo of the Fort and King streets corner was taken after 1912, but the exact year and date is unknown.

It looks like a street in some small country town, but this scene was captured by the camera in 1872 on upper Nuuanu Street near Kuakini Street.   Robert E. Van Dyke Col

Robert E. Van Dyke Collection

This rather ramshackle establishment stood at the corner of Alakea and King about 1895, with its sign already advertising the advantages of a resort.

Old Honolulu

Aliiolani Hale was constructed in 1872-74 and was originally planned as a palace for Hawaii's royalty. King Kalakaua dedicated the statue of King Kamehameha I, which now stands in front of the building, on Febuary 14, 1883. Today this handsome building serves as the State Judiciary Building.

This building at Hotel and Richards Streets was the original Royal Hawaiian Hotel. The photo was taken in 1875. Today this site is the location of the Armed Forces YMCA. The new Royal Hawaiian Hotel opened in Waikiki in February, 1927.

The photo above shows the August Ahrens residence at the corner of Wilder and Piikoi Streets in 1906. Below is shown the same corner residence in 1937, by which time the trolley had been replaced by buses. As of this printing in 1978, the house still stands, though in bad shape.

Residence of Princess Ruth Keelikolani, now the site of Central Intermediate School.

Robert E. Van Dyke Collection

Old Honolulu

Steamer Day

Continuing a custom that began with the visit of Captain Cook, the arrival of any large ship at Honolulu Harbor was always a cause for joy and expectation. One never knew what the ship might bring — mail, unexpected friends, a long-awaited cargo. It soon became a tradition to greet ships as they pulled into the dock, particularly after the advent of steam power inaugurated an era of dependable scheduled service.

Before long, the greeting began to take on a more ceremonial aspect. The Royal Hawaiian Band enlivened the events with stirring martial airs and sentimental tunes of greeting and farewell. Word was passed as soon as the lookout on Diamond Head spotted an arriving steamer. Fleets of yachts and boats went out to escort the steamer into the harbor, and there would later be on-boat parties for passengers, crews and greeters.

Among the many picturesque dockside sights on Steamer Day were the lines of Hawaiian lei sellers stringing flowers of a hundred varieties in every possible combination and vending their floral wares to greeters and the newly arrived as well as those departing. On departing steamers there grew a tradition of throwing one's lei overboard as the ship left the harbor. If the leis drifted back to shore (as they usually did) it meant that one would return.

Steamer Day about 1915. The steamer has arrived and the dockside street is alive with hurrying greeters and floral lei vendors.

Baker Photo, Bishop Museum

Old Honolulu

Lei Sellers

Lei sellers vend their colorful creations on a downtown sidewalk in the early 1900's. Business was especially brisk on Steamer Day as residents rushed to buy greeting leis for newly arrived visitors.

Old Honolulu

Royal Hawaiian Band

Captain Henry Berger, founder and leader for many years, stands in front of the Royal Hawaiian Band. No major event in old Honolulu was complete without a performance by this popular band. This famed band has played all over the world and has survived through the overthrow of the monarchy, annexation and statehood. To this day its performances all over the state are enjoyed by all of Hawaii's people. It still performs every Friday in the bandstand on the grounds of Iolani Palace, on the spot where King Kalakaua was crowned, just a few yards from the site of this photo.

Surfing

Surfing has spread a long way from its original Hawaii home. Dedicated enthusiasts crowd surfing spots in all the warm seas of the globe and even in certain cold-water areas.

There are indications that body surfing (without a surfboard) was known on many islands in Polynesia, and that a primitive form of surfboarding may even have been enjoyed in Tahiti and the other Society Islands. But surfing as a sport came into full flower in ancient Hawaii.

Like other aspects of life in old Hawaii, surfing was imbued with spiritual significance. A Hawaiian did not simply sit down and make a surfboard. Selecting the proper tree, cutting it, shaping and preparing the wood—each step had its rituals and ceremonies deemed necessary so that the gods would grant success to the board and its owner. The launching of the board into the sea for the first time was done with the appropriate ritual.

There were two kinds of surfboards in use in old Hawaii, a short board called the "alaia" and a longer one known as the "olo." The short "alaia" was used by women and children in riding the waves closer to shore while the "olo" was ridden in the big waves further out. Generally, the smaller "alaia" boards were made of koa or breadfruit wood which was heavy compared to the light wiliwili wood of the long "olo" boards.

It was typical of the hierarchical society of old Hawaii that the common people could not use the more satisfactory wiliwili wood for their surfboards but had to be content with the heavy and less buoyant koa. One result was that the alii became the best surfers. The alii had better boards and they put a kapu on the best surfing beaches. Also, the alii were larger and stronger than the general population and had more leisure to develop their physique and their surfing skills.

The old surfboards were bigger, heavier and more difficult to handle. They did not have the skeg, which is a little rudder at the stern found on today's boards. Some of the ancient boards in museum collections are eighteen feet or more in length and weigh more than 150 pounds.

After the arrival of the missionaries in 1820, surfing went into a steep decline and almost disappeared as a sport. The missionaries considered surfing to be a waste of valuable time better spent in work or prayer.

In 1874, when King Kalakaua ascended the throne of Hawaii, surfing became popular again, but after his death the sport of surfing once more almost disappeared. But in the early 1900's as Hawaii's economy improved, there was an increase of interest in sports. What had originally been purely a Hawaiian sport was taken up by young people of all backgrounds. Canoe and surfing clubs were formed and enthusiasm spread. Soon the waters off Waikiki were crowded with young people enjoying surfing and improving their skills on the waves.

Archives, State of Hawaii

Early visitors to the Hawaiian Islands were amazed to see men, women and children astride long wooden planks defying and mastering huge breakers as they raced shoreward. In those days it was a spectacle to be seen nowhere else in the world. Today Hawaii's unique sport of surfing attracts fanatic devotees wherever wave conditions and temperature allow.

Surfing

Duke Kahanamoku

The individual who must be given the most credit for the renaissance of surfing was Duke Kahanamoku. In 1912, this handsome Hawaiian swimming athlete startled the world when, as a member of the American Swimming Team, he smashed the record for the 100-meter dash at the Olympics in Stockholm.

Wherever he went, Duke demonstrated the Hawaiian sport of surfing to fascinated crowds. In Australia, California, and on the Atlantic Coast he won thousands of converts who began building their own boards and, after they had mastered the art, experimenting with new techniques of surfing and board construction.

After a temporary decline during World War II, surfing took another upsurge in the 1950's. Light balsa-wood boards soon replaced the heavy and clumsy redwood boards that had previously been common. Innovators were constantly improving board designs, seeking lightness and maneuverability. Today's surfboards are fairly standardized in design and size, falling in the six to eight foot length category according to the size and weight of the owner.

Hawaii is now the scene for many worldwide surfing competitions, held particularly in the mountainous surf of the North Shore and Makaha areas of Oahu. Every year, surfing greats from everywhere compete in the Duke Kahanamoku Invitational Surfing Championship Meet, named in honor of the great Hawaiian sportsman who did so much to rescue his people's ancient sport from oblivion.

Hawaii Visitors Bur•

Well into late middle age, Duke remained in top form as a surfer. When he died, his ashes were scattered from an outrigger canoe into the surf he loved so well.

Camera Hawaii photograph by Werner Stoy

As Hawaii's Official Greeter, Duke Kahanamoku welcomed prominent visitors from all over the world. Duke's outgoing personality made even the most reserved feel at home. Queen Mother Elizabeth of Great Britain was so charmed by the Duke's infectious gaiety that she joined him in an impromptu hula, to the delight of one and all.

Only the boldest challenge the giant waves on Oahu's North Shore.

Hawaii Visitors Bureau

Canoe Racing

Hawaiian outrigger canoe racing grows in popularity every year with old and new canoe clubs competing for honors in the many races held throughout the State.

Spectators crowd the beaches at the finish of an outrigger canoe race, ready to cheer the victors and partake of the fun and excitement.

A.

Waikiki

It was once a long sandspit with its front on the ocean and, at its back, a swampy lowland dotted with rice paddies, taro patches and duck ponds. The place was called Waikiki, a favorite retreat where old-time Hawaiians came to relax and enjoy life.

Those who knew Waikiki a few years ago hardly recognize the place today. The few posh old "grande-dame" hotels like the Royal Hawaiian, the Moana and the Halekulani are almost lost in the maze of modern high-rises that have proliferated like mushrooms.

There are many who bemoan the passing of the "old Waikiki" and its replacement by concrete canyons that block the sights that visitors come to see — Diamond Head and the ocean. The old Waikiki was quiet and languid, a place where time was a matter of small import.

Today things are different. Waikiki is still a place where one can enjoy a lazy, relaxing day wherein "doing things" is not allowed to interfere with the pleasures of loafing on the beach or beside the pool. But, for those of a more energetic persuasion, Waikiki today pulsates with vitality and excitement, with old-fashioned hula shows, hip-mod discotheques, Vegas-type showrooms and gourmet restaurants.

Kalakaua Avenue (Waikiki Road) about 1898.　　　　　Bishop Museum

Waikiki

Archives, State of

The Moiliili section of Honolulu, inland from Waikiki, once an area of extensive rice paddies and taro patches is today a highly urbanized neighborhood.

Diamond Head view from McCully Tract. A bucolic landscape with taro patches, rice paddies, farm houses and a lone coconut tree. That's how it was captured on film in 1910. Today, this same location, near King and McCully streets, is a heavily populated residential neighborhood of single-family homes interspersed with low-rise apartment buildings.

This peaceful beach scene, looking toward Diamond Head, was taken long before Waikiki became the mecca of Hawaii's visitors. In those simpler days it was a quiet strip of coconut-palm-lined beach. Hawaiian royalty and well-to-do citizens kept beach cottages in Waikiki as hideaways from the cares of everyday life.

In 1884 this view was captured of a site near the present foot of Kapahulu Avenue, presently the site of Kuhio Beach in Waikiki. In those days a small stream entered the ocean about a block past these fishermen preparing their canoe and nets.

Waikiki

In 1902, a trip to Waikiki was a happy outing in this quaint trolley. The picture was taken at the juncture of McCully and Kalakaua. This area was still devoted to banana, rice and taro patches. The Moana Hotel is barely visible in the distance below the crest of Diamond Head.

Believe it or not, this photo was taken on the site of what is now the Royal Hawaiian Hotel. Waikiki has certainly changed since then. This grass shack was located in the country estate of King Kamehameha V at Waikiki and was probably used for the living quarters of his native Hawaiian retainers. The king himself lived in a large wooden dwelling closer to the beach.

Waikiki

The Moana Hotel in the early 1900's.

Bishop Mu

Waikiki, early 1930's. The major structure is the Royal Hawaiian Hotel which opened in February 1927.

Archives, State of Hawaii

Waikiki

Hawaii Calls

All the nostalgic appeal of the "Hawaii Calls" radio show is captured in this photo from the 1930's. The girl in the hat is the beloved Hilo Hattie.

There must be millions of Americans who, as children in the 1930's and 1940's, remember tuning in to a radio program named "Hawaii Calls." They would await that thrilling opening moment when the soft wash of the surf on the beach and the haunting sound of the conch-shell trumpet could be heard. The swaying palms, the sandy beach, the blue sky, and the colorfully costumed Hawaiian singers gathered on the shore could be seen in the mind, stimulated by "the magic of radio." More than anything else, "Hawaii Calls" was responsible for popularizing Hawaiian music on the mainland and in other parts of the world, where it was heard by shortwave radio.

The music played on the program was known as "hapa-haole," or half-white, music. These were songs sung in a Hawaiian style consisting of mostly English words with a few Hawaiian words thrown in for spice and color. Some, including "Sweet Leilani" and "My Little Grass Shack," became world famous. The program and its performers presented the kind of Hawaiian entertainment that they felt the outside world wanted to hear. Often the performers sang Hawaiian songs in the Hawaiian language, but the overall emphasis was on the hapa-haole music so popular at the time. Many Hawaiian entertainers got their start on "Hawaii Calls" and later went off to show business fame on their own.

Today, Hawaiian music is undergoing a renaissance with Hawaiian music of the countryside becoming more popular than ever with local residents. Slack-key guitar and Hawaiian folk songs form the major components of concerts given by today's musicians. In Waikiki nightclubs and at commercial luaus for visitors, however, the music tends to follow the older trend, offering the hapa-haole songs the average visitor expects to hear.

Waikiki

Modern Waikiki, center of Hawaii's visitor industry.

Star Bulletin Photo by Warren R. Roll

Honolulu Star-Bulletin 1st EXTRA

Evening Bulletin, Est. 1882, No. 11374
Hawaiian Star, Vol. XLVIII, No. 15330

8 PAGES—HONOLULU, TERRITORY OF HAWAII, U. S. A., SUNDAY, DECEMBER 7, 1941—8 PAGES

★ PRICE FIVE CENTS

WAR !

(Associated Press by Transpacific Telephone)

SAN FRANCISCO, Dec. 7.—President Roosevelt announced this morning that Japanese planes had attacked Manila and Pearl Harbor.

OAHU BOMBED BY JAPANESE PLANES

SIX KNOWN DEAD, 21 INJURED, AT EMERGENCY HOSPITAL

Attack Made On Island's Defense Areas

By UNITED PRESS

WASHINGTON, Dec. 7.—Text of a White House announcement detailing the attack on the Hawaiian islands is:

"The Japanese attacked Pearl Harbor from the air and all naval and military activities on the island of Oahu, principal American base in the Hawaiian islands."

Oahu was attacked at 7:55 this morning by Japanese planes.

The Rising Sun, emblem of Japan, was seen on plane wing tips.

Wave after wave of bombers streamed through the clouded morning sky from the southwest and flung their missiles on a city resting in peaceful Sabbath calm.

According to an unconfirmed report received at the governor's office, the Japanese force that attacked Oahu reached island waters aboard two small airplane carriers.

It was also reported that at the governor's

CIVILIANS ORDERED OFF STREETS

The army has ordered that all civilians stay off the streets and highways and not use telephones.

Evidence that the Japanese attack has registered some hits was shown by three billowing pillars of smoke in the Pearl Harbor and Hickam field area.

All navy personnel and civilian defense workers, with the exception of women, have been ordered to duty at Pearl Harbor.

The Pearl Harbor highway was immediately a mass of racing cars.

A trickling stream of injured people began pouring into the city emergency hospital a few minutes after the bombardment started.

Thousands of telephone calls almost swamped the Mutual Telephone Co., which put extra operators on duty.

At The Star-Bulletin office the phone calls deluged the single operator and it was impossible for this newspaper, for sometime, to handle the flood of calls. Here also an emergency operator was called.

HOUR OF ATTACK—7:55 A. M.

An official army report from department headquarters, made public shortly before 11, is that the first attack was at 7:55 a. m.

Witnesses said they saw at least 50 airplanes over Pearl Harbor.

ANTIAIRCRAFT GUNS IN ACTION

First indication of the raid came shortly before 8 this morning when antiaircraft guns around Pearl Habor began sending up a thunderous barrage.

At the same time a vast cloud of black smoke arose from the naval base and also from Hickam field where flames could be seen.

BOMB NEAR GOVERNOR'S MANSION

Shortly before 9:30 a bomb fell near Washington Place, the residence of the governor, Governor Poindexter and Secretary Charles M. Hite were there.

It was reported that the bomb killed an unidentified Chinese man across the street in front of the Schuman Carriage Co. where windows were broken.

C. E. Daniels, a welder, found a fragment of shell or bomb at South and Queen Sts. which he brought into the City Hall. This fragrant weighed about a pound.

At 10:05 a. m. today Governor Poindexter telephoned to The Star-Bulletin announcing he has declared a state of emergency for the entire territory.

He announced that Edouard L. Doty, executive secretary of the major disaster council, has been appointed director under the M-Day law's provisions.

Governor Poindexter urged all residents of

Hundreds See City Bombed

Hundreds of Honolulans who hurried to the top of Punchbowl soon after bombs began to fall, saw spread out before them the whole panorama of surprise attack and defense.

Far off over Pearl Harbor the white sky was polka-dotted with anti-aircraft smoke.

Rolling away from the navy base were billowing clouds of ugly black smoke. Sometimes a burst of flame reddened the black sources of the smoke.

Out from the silver-surfaced mouth of the harbor a flotilla of destroyers streamed in battle, smoke pouring from their stacks.

Turn to Page 2, Column 2

Schools Closed

All schools on Oahu, both public and private, will remain closed until further notice, Edouard L. Doty, territorial director of civilian defense, announced at 11 a. m. today. This does not apply elsewhere in the territory.

Names of Dead and Injured

The city emergency hospital reported at 10:30 a list of 6 killed and 21 injured.

The complete list will be carried later. Here is a partial list:

Peter Lopes, 34, of 3461 Kaumakili St., was reported at 9:30 a. m. to be in serious condition from wounds in the upper abdomen.

Bernice Gouveia, 37, 2708 KaMoi St. is suffering from a mangled thigh, lacerations on the right leg and left arm.

A Portuguese girl, unidentified, 10 years old, died on arrival from puncture wounds.

Another victim who died on arrival was Frank Ohashi, 33, 3745 Kaumakili St., from puncture wounds in the chest.

Cecelia Broadly, 38, Moanalua gardens, was released from the hospital after treatment for lacerations.

Three were reported injured and one reported killed from the bomb that fell at Fort and School Sts.

Editorial

HAWAII MEETS THE CRISIS

100

World War II

Pearl Harbor

Aircraft destroyed on the ground at Ford Island in Pearl Harbor. In the background, the smoke and flames of giant battleships destroyed at their berths.

World War II

Pearl Harbor

A powerful giant, the U. S. S. Arizona, keels over in its death agony, sinking at its berth after the Japanese attack.

U. S

World War II

Pearl Harbor

The Pearl Harbor disaster ranks as one of the major events in American and Hawaiian history. Controversy remains as to why our forces were caught so completely by surprise in spite of numerous indications that trouble with Japan was imminent. Even the Imperial Japanese Admiralty had hardly expected such a complete destruction of America's naval power in the Pacific.

In one hour and fifty minutes the attacking carrier-based planes managed to destroy virtually the entire American Pacific Fleet. Even though the Japanese planes had been detected by radar when they were more than a hundred miles away, no general alarm had been sounded. The received signal at first was thought to have been reflected from American carrier-based planes on maneuvers or from a flight of bombers expected from the mainland. When the attacking planes came in over Kolekole Pass to slide down toward Pearl Harbor, the Japanese pilots could hardly believe that their arrival was a total surprise. Not an anti-aircraft gun was firing, not a fighter plane was in the air to challenge them.

Eight huge battleships, impressive dreadnaughts of the sea, were either sunk or damaged during the Japanese attack. Only the U.S.S. Nevada managed to get under way and she too eventually was run aground under severe bombing attack. Three light cruisers were seriously damaged, three destroyers and four lesser vessels suffered the same fate as the giants on Battleship Row off Ford Island. American planes damaged or destroyed, mostly on the ground, totalled 347. The U.S. military death toll was 2,251.

The Japanese attack on Pearl Harbor, aside from its destructiveness, had an impact on Hawaii's history almost as great as Captain Cook's arrival 163 years before. Until December 7, 1941, Hawaii had slumbered on quietly, dominated by the plantation economy and a monolithic business establishment almost completely in the hands of a few interlocking corporations. Each major racial group kept roughly to its assigned "place" or occupational category.

The aftermath of Pearl Harbor, with its tremendous influx of soldiers and workers (and radical ideas) from the mainland, would change that. Hawaii's sons in uniform, often only one generation removed from the plantations, received an invaluable education about the U.S. and other parts of the world. They returned home determined to participate fully in Hawaii's society.

The U. S. S. Arizona Memorial at Pearl Harbor, built over the hull of the sunken battleship.

U. S. Navy

Hawaii's Very Special Regiment

Hawaii's 442nd off to the war in a ceremony at Iolani Palace on March 28, 1943.

Hawaii's Very Special Regiment

The Japanese attack on Pearl Harbor caused immediate trouble for America's citizens of Japanese ancestry. Those on the mainland were quickly dispossessed and moved to so-called relocation camps. But, what was to be done about the 160,000 Japanese in Hawaii, most of whom were citizens? They could hardly be sent to camps on the mainland since there were simply not enough ships available, not to mention the impracticality of interning one-third of the entire population of Hawaii.

Hawaii's Japanese-Americans were patriotic citizens, a fact that became apparent once the initial hysteria died down. Still, suspicion lingered on.

The military were uncomfortable with the possibility of a Japanese invasion of the Hawaiian islands at the time when there were some 1,300 Americans of Japanese Ancestry (AJA's) on duty in Hawaii's two National Guard Battalions. To discharge all of the AJA's was a military luxury not to be afforded at a time when manpower was at a premium. The solution was to form the Hawaiian Provisional Infantry Battalion composed of 1,406 Nisei soldiers to be trained outside the islands.

During the Battle of Midway they were sent to Camp McCoy in Wisconsin where they were treated with considerable friendliness by people of the nearby towns. Later, however, they were transferred to Camp Shelby in Mississippi, where racial hostility toward them at times was intense because of their "color." The Hawaiian Provisional Infantry Battalion was renamed the 100th Battalion and, after training, the Battalion was sent first to North Africa and then to Italy.

Later the War Department authorized the formation of an all-AJA fighting unit and put out a call for Hawaii volunteers in early 1943.

The original appeal was for 1,500 volunteers, but within a month over 9,000 young AJA's flocked to recruitment centers in Hawaii. Some 2,645 were selected to serve and they formed the core of the 442nd Infantry Regiment. On June 11, 1944, they joined the 100th Battalion north of Rome and eventually absorbed that unit.

The combat record of these young Japanese-Americans is unequalled in the annals of American military history. They fought valiantly in Italy and France. Their casualty rate was three times higher than the average. The combined units won seven Presidential Unit Citations and nearly 6,000 other medals were awarded to individual soldiers.

The men of the 442nd returned to Hawaii as a new kind of citizen of the islands. They had traveled, they had seen much and suffered much. They would not be content to let things go on in the old way, wherein the decision-making process remained in the hands of an elite oligarchy. They would enter politics and help transform Hawaii into a new and exciting place where all men had their say in the decisions that would shape Hawaii's future.

The Military

From a military point of view, Hawaii's strategic location had long made the islands a desirable acquisition. Ships of the U.S. Navy had called regularly throughout the nineteenth century and the Navy saw Pearl Harbor as a potential naval base. Annexation became more urgent when it was suddenly recognized that Hawaii was an important halfway point for refreshing troops on their way to combat in the Philippines during the Spanish-American War and the ensuing nationalist insurrections. Negotiations proceeded at full speed and American soldiers were actually on the way from California before the official annexation date of August 12, 1898, arriving in Hawaii on August 16.

The Army. The first U.S. Army encampment was set up at a site in Kapiolani Park when infantry and engineer elements paused here en route to the Philippines. It was called Camp McKinley, the only military establishment in the Territory until 1907, when Fort Shafter was built.

With annexation, the Army was faced with the task of defending the new Territory. In 1908, work was begun on a new major military post on the Leilehua plateau of central Oahu. This post was named Schofield Barracks to honor Civil War Lt. Gen. John M. Schofield, who had earlier visited Hawaii and recommended the acquisition of Pearl Harbor for the Navy. Wheeler Field, at the south end of Schofield, was established by the Army Air Corps in 1922. Construction of Hickam Field began in 1935. Later, the Army Air Corps became a separate branch of service, the Air Force.

The Navy. The first U.S. Navy ship to visit Hawaii anchored in Honolulu Harbor in 1826. Some 25 years before annexation, the Navy built a coaling station in Honolulu. Construction of the giant naval complex began in 1909 and the U.S.S. *California* became the first U.S. warship to enter Pearl Harbor in 1911.

The Marines. The Marine Corps first moved into Pearl Harbor barracks in 1923, and in 1953 the former Naval Air Station at Kaneohe was recommissioned as a Marine Corps Air Station.

The Coast Guard. Coast Guard cutters have been patrolling Hawaiian waters since the Spanish-American War. Today the Hawaii-based Coast Guard supervises a vast area of the central Pacific, ranging as far as Alaska and Samoa.

World War I. Hawaii and the military forces stationed here played a minor part in the affairs of World War I. Nine German naval vessels were seized upon the outbreak of hostilities between Germany and the U.S. Those vessels had previously sought sanctuary here from the Japanese Navy in 1914 during America's period of neutrality.

World War II and Afterwards. By the late '30's it became obvious that the U.S. and Japan would have a showdown in the Pacific and so the military establishment in Hawaii grew larger with every passing year. On December 7, 1941, martial law was declared and Hawaii remained under military rule until October 19, 1944. Though there was no real need for such a lengthy period of military control, it took that long for the civilian establishment to regain its control over Hawaii's affairs. Life under martial law was difficult, as most normal civil rights were suspended. The press was heavily censored, especially the two Japanese-American dailies that were allowed to continue. Wages of all workers were frozen and work absenteeism was punishable by jail sentence.

During both the Korean and Vietnam conflicts, the islands served as a staging area. During the Vietnam War, Hawaii was a popular rest-and-recuperation center for the troops involved. Today, defense represents a major industry for Hawaii is the nation's Pacific bastion of defense. Recent Defense Department downsizing has not greatly impacted Hawaii, although Oahu's Barbers Point Naval Air Station may close.

Bishop Museum

Army supply wagons drawn by four-mule teams pass in review at Schofield Barracks in the 1930's.

Ships of the Pacific Fleet at Pearl Harbor were often welcomed in a way similar to this scene taken in 1950. Here the crew is eagerly eyeing the hula dancers, some of whom wear cellophane "grass" skirts popular in hula shows of that time.

The Neighbor Islands

Most of the significant events during the last two centuries of Hawaiian history have occurred on the island of Oahu. There were good reasons for this. Oahu, with its excellent harbor facilities and the port of Honolulu, almost at once became the shipping and business hub as none of the other islands offered such ample and sheltered harbors.

During the long centuries before the arrival of Captain Cook, each major island was a separate kingdom and no one island was really more important than another. But once the islands had been united as a kingdom by Kamehameha The Great, the situation changed completely. There was a need for one central place of authority,

and Honolulu on the island of Oahu fulfilled all the requirements.

The early Hawaiian monarchy maintained the capital at Kailua-Kona on the island of Hawaii. Later they shifted it to Lahaina on Maui. However, it was soon apparent that the ideal location would be Honolulu if the rulers were to keep abreast of all the fast moving developments affecting the kingdom. With its growing importance as a business and population center, Honolulu was the obvious choice as a capital of the islands.

Today the island of Oahu far surpasses the other islands in population and commercial activity. Its density exceeds that of Japan and England with almost 718,400

persons residing in only 604 square miles.

Nevertheless, it is on the other islands where the more leisurely life of olden days still maintains a stronghold. Here the old dream is more alive, and the urban hustle and bustle of Honolulu can be left behind. Once, the population of the islands was fairly evenly distributed but Oahu now serves as home to about eighty percent of the state's total population. Long outside the mainstream of Hawaiian history, the neighbor islands slumber on in comparative tranquility, symbols of the quiet and gentle way of living that typified the past, although that too is being threatened with change in the wake of tourist development.

In 1939, this section of the Big Island's Hamakua Coast was heavily planted with taro. Taro root was the staple of the Hawaiian diet when mashed into poi. It was as important to the Hawaiians as was the potato to the Irish.

The Neighbor Islands

KAUAI

Kauai, lying about 103 statute miles slightly northwest of Honolulu, is the most remote of the major Hawaiian islands. Historically, it was the last of the individual island kingdoms to become part of the united Hawaiian kingdom. When Kamehameha The Great had conquered all of the other islands, he planned to add Kauai to his dominions, but a storm dispersed his invasion fleet. Eventually, Kauai submitted to the rule of Kamehameha voluntarily.

NIIHAU

Seventeen miles west of Kauai's southwestern shore lies the island of Niihau, whose 230 pure-Hawaiian inhabitants speak Hawaiian as their first language. Known as the "Forbidden Island," Niihau has been an isolated pocket of old Hawaii. However, in the early 1990s helicopter tours began to land on deserted stretches of the 72-square-mile isle. Visitors can go on hunting safaris, but are forbidden on inhabited parts of the island, owned by the Robinson family for more than 130 years.

MOLOKAI

While the island of Molokai is easily visible from lookout points on Oahu's eastern shore, it is years removed in mood and way of life. A large part of its population of about 6,700 is of Hawaiian or part-Hawaiian blood who live a quiet life of fishing, farming and hunting. For long centuries, Molokai was known as The Lonely Island. As it does today, it had a comparatively small population and Molokai's kahunas (priests of the ancient Hawaiian religion) were feared for their great powers. Molokai was also the site of the leper colony at Kalaupapa on its northern shore, isolated from outside contact by brooding cliffs and dangerous surf.

MAUI

Maui, the second largest of Hawaii's major islands, with an area of 728 square miles, is named after the Polynesian demi-god, Maui. According to legend, he pulled the Hawaiian Islands up from the bottom of the sea with his fish hook. In another story about Maui, he caused the sun to slow its journey over the islands so that there would be more time for drying tapa cloth.

The island of Maui was formed when two adjacent volcanoes, Haleakala (which means house of the sun) and the West Maui mountains, grew together at their bases as their peaks rose higher above the sea. The West Maui mountains are somewhat older than Haleakala and endless centuries of erosion have sculpted dramatic green valleys into their flanks.

LANAI

The third smallest of Hawaii's inhabited islands, Lanai lies 50 miles southeast of Honolulu and nine miles off the west coast of Maui. The 141-square-mile isle is part of Maui County. Its population of about 2,400 people lives mainly in the town of Lanai City. Lanai had been known as the "Pineapple Island," once being the world's largest source of pineapples, but in the 1980s the island moved away from pineapple and towards tourism as its economic mainstay. Two upscale resorts at Keole now employ most of the work force of the island. Pineapple grows on only 100 acres.

HAWAII—The Big Island

The island of Hawaii is the largest and geologically youngest of all the Hawaiian islands. It is still growing as volcanic eruptions in recent years have added hundreds of acres of new land.

Hawaii has the tallest mountains in the state - both Mauna Kea and Mauna Loa approach to nearly 14,000 feet above sea level. It is 4,038 square miles in area - twice the combined size of all the other islands - and has a population of about 120,300. The climate, as befits such a large and high island, varies considerably, from lush rain forests to deserts. On the two highest peaks, snow covers the summits for several months each winter. At Kealakekua Bay Captain Cook met his end. Hawaii was also the home base for Kamehameha as he united all the islands into one kingdom. Starting in the 1980s a series of luxurious mega-resorts was built on the Big Island.

Robert E. Van Dyke Collection

A scene of downtown Hilo's waterfront area taken in 1878. On April 1, 1946, Hilo's waterfront area was devastated by a giant tidal wave which caused many fatalities and enormous damage.

The Neighbor Islands

Tidal Waves

Tidal waves are a fact of life in the islands and continental seashores bordering the Pacific Ocean. They occur in all oceans but are especially prevalent in the Pacific, which contains more regions of volcanic action than anywhere else on earth. When earthquakes occur under the sea bottom, they often cause the formation of fast-moving waves that travel rapidly outward. At sea, these resultant waves are hardly distinguishable from normal ocean waves, but as they approach land they may build up, inundating coastal areas and sweeping everything in their path.

In recent years, Hawaii has often suffered devastation from such tidal waves, or tsunamis as they are called in Japan where the study of volcanism and tidal waves is pursued dilligently. On each occasion, the worst loss of lives and property damage was suffered on the Big Island, though destruction was considerable elsewhere in the islands. Some people, washed out to sea, survived by clinging to floating debris. On November 29, 1975, a combination earthquake, tidal wave and volcanic eruption caused a fatality and much property damage. Parts of the coastline sank beneath the sea.

The Hawaiian Islands are the products of volcanic activity that began about 18 million years ago when lava crept through a fault or crack in the earth's surface and began building mountains beneath the sea. Through eons of time the undersea mounts grew until they rose above the waves. On the Big Island of Hawaii, Mauna Kea and Mauna Loa tower nearly 14,000 feet above sea level, starting from a base 18,000 feet below the surface.

As the islands grew, they were worn down by the action of waves, rain, sun and wind. Soil formed and life appeared, clothing the islands in greenery. On every island but the Big Island of Hawaii, there came a time when the volcanoes ceased their eruptions. The balance tipped and the slow wearing down process continued

EXTRA

TIDAL WAVES CRASH HILO

Honolulu Star-Bulletin

20 PAGES—HONOLULU, T. H., U. S. A. MONDAY, APRIL 1, 1946—20 PAGES

★★★ AIRPLANE DELIVERY ON ISLANDS OTHER THAN OAHU 7¢ PRICE ON OAHU 5¢

LATE NEWS FINAL

Damage Done by the Waves at the Ala Wai Yacht Harbor

20 Dead Reported In The Territory And Toll May Grow

The Sea As It Receded At Waikiki Near The Elks Club

Aleutian Quake Is Blamed

No Authentic Reports Of Second Wave

without repair.

The oldest islands, once high, green, lovely lands, are nearly stripped down to their basalt bases. They are now rock and coral outcroppings barely projecting above sea level.

Hawaii, newest of the islands, is still growing. The volcanoes of Mauna Loa and Kilauea continue to pour forth their immense quantities of lava. When lava reaches the sea, it can add acres of new land. Yet, over the long, slow ages of geological time, the present high islands will weather away, possibly to be replaced by new islands. According to a recent theory called "plate tectonics" or "continental drift," the leeward islands once stood where the Island of Hawaii stands today. They have since "drifted" westward to their present positions. In a never-ending process, what the sea and rain take from Hawaii, the volcanoes give back.

The Neighbor Islands

Madame Pele: The Volcano Goddess

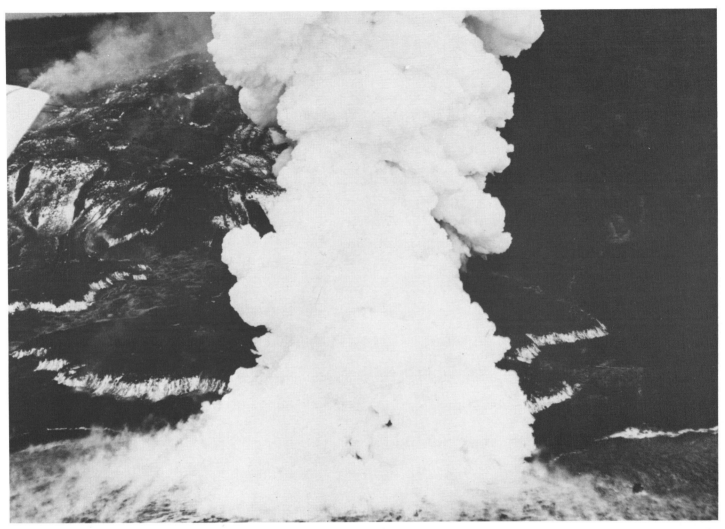

Hot lava pours into the ocean. Thus, the island of Hawaii grows.

Hawaii Visitors Bureau

Her home is a region of natural wonders and stark contrasts where dripping-wet rain forests shelter primeval giant tree-ferns. With almost shocking abruptness, the dim emerald shade gives way to sun-blasted lava lands that appear never to have known a drop of rain. Steam clouds rise from fumaroles and drift through the forest like disembodied spirits. The bright sunshine of day is counterpointed by the misty silence of night. During eruptions, the quiet darkness is shattered by the rumble and hiss of lava gushing from fiery reservoirs beneath the earth. Lowering clouds glow with the crimson reflection of liquid rock fountaining hundreds of feet into the air.

This is Volcano Country on the Big Island of Hawaii, home of Pele, the volcano goddess. In this otherworldly region Pele's eerie presence is as real as in the heyday of her rule over the people of Hawaii. Of all ancient Hawaii's gods, only Pele continued to live in the hearts of the Hawaiian people after the spontaneous overthrow of their own religion in 1819. To this day, she is honored both secretly and openly by Hawaiians of all classes who remain loyal to their temperamental volcano mistress and her spectacular displays of flaming wrath.

Hurricane Iniki

America's Third Worst Natural Disaster

Hurricane Iniki battered Kauai on September 11, 1992, with sustained winds of 145 miles per hour and gusts of up to 227 mph. Eight people died of storm-related causes, 332 were injured, 21,000 homes were damaged, and more than a billion dollars' damage was done. Eight thousand of Kauai's 50,000 people were left homeless. Agricultural losses were estimated at $150 million.

As Iniki sped towards the islands, it was originally feared it might hit Oahu, but damage to Oahu was relatively light—$25.7 million—confined mostly to

Weather details, A4

TODAY'S OUTLOOK: Mostly sunny with occasional showers

NEWS SUMMARY ON PAGE A2

SPORTS

'Bows go 2-0, face BYU next

— Page C1

HURRICANE INIKI

At least four people are dead.	Damage could reach $1 billion.
Two boaters may be lost at sea.	Kauai destruction is islandwide.
Scores are injured on Kauai.	Chunks of Na Pali coast wash into sea.

Sunday

HONOLULU September 13, 1992

Star-Bulletin & Advertiser
Final Edition $1.50

'It broke my heart'

The Honolulu Advertiser, Bruce Asato

The devastation wrought by Hurrican Iniki. While property damage was great, there was little loss of life. Mother nature can wreck havoc on the Hawaiian Islands which are fragile to acts of nature. Hawaii's history includes tidal waves, tsunamis, hurricanes, volcanic eruptions and bomb attacks. Earthquakes have caused little damage.

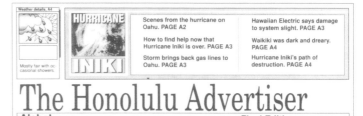

The Honolulu Advertiser, Richard Ambo

the Waianae Coast on Oahu's northwestern shore, the closest part of the island to Kauai. Although Waikiki Beach disappeared under turbulent seas during the storm, Honolulu was spared major destruction. If the hurricane had hit Hawaii's most populated and urbanized island full force, the result may have been catastrophic.

Natural disasters such as Hurricane Iniki show the vulnerability of the Hawaiian archipelago to the forces of nature. Besides hurricanes, there have been numerous volcanic eruptions on the Big Island, particularly since 1983, causing massive uncontrollable lava flows. Fortunately, there has been no loss of life, although villages and subdi-

visions had to be abandoned. On the optimistic side, new lands, and even a new Hawaiian island, are being created by Madame Pele's volcano.

Mankind can also be a threatening force to the islands. Hawaii has the highest number of endangered (282) and threatened (161) species of flora and fauna of any of the states.

STATEHOOD!

House Sends Bill to Ike

WASHINGTON, D.C., March 12—Congress ended decades of procrastination today and sent to the White House a bill to give Hawaii the Statehood it has so long deserved.

The House overwhelmingly approved the bill this afternoon.

The vote was 323-89. The time was 3:04 p.m. E.S.T. (10:04 a.m. H.S.T.). It was the same bill that passed the Senate 76-15 last night.

The House action sent the bill on to President Eisenhower whose signature was assured.

The actual admission will be delayed for several months by the mechanics of procedure which includes holding an election in Hawaii.

It likely will be late July, possibly as late as October, before the 50th State formally joins the Union.

President Eisenhower has 10 legislative days —not counting Sundays —to sign the bill after it formally is presented to him, possibly tomorrow.

Under the terms of the bill, the Governor of Hawaii has 30 days after formal notification of the President's approval to issue a proclamation of elections.

More Statehood . . .

On Pages 1-A, 1-B

Whig Paper Urged Statehood in 1849

Many Changes Due In Status of Isles

Statehood Won OK's Four Times Before

Statehood Reasons Given Over Years

State Offices Lure Politicians

. . . On the Inside

Question on Size Of State . . . Page 1-D

Two New Songs Mark Statehood . . . Page 5

Burns Eyes Senate Post . . . Page 1-D

Celebrations Sweep Honolulu . . . Page 2-A

Resolution Favors 'Aloha State' . . . Page 21

Governors Laud Isles . . . Page 5

The primary election could be held no less than 60 or more than 90 days after the proclamation. A general election could be held no later than 40 days after the primary.

After the results of the elections are officially certified to the President—assuming Hawaii elects to accept Statehood—the President would issue his proclamation admitting Hawaii as a state.

Governor Quinn of Hawaii said today he was not prepared to say how soon he could be ready to proclaim elections or what time interval would be allowed for them.

As the House roll call reached the 218 affirmative votes needed for passage, Governor Quinn, who was waiting here, telephoned a signal for celebrations to be touched off in Hawaii. This was about 2:57 p.m. (9:57 a.m. Hawaii Time.)

It was a moment the residents of the last incorporated territory under the American flag had awaited for more than 50 years.

Hawaii will be the first island state. But Alaska's admission as the 49th state had already broken through a long argument from some Congress members against admitting territories not joined geographically to the other states.

Congressional opposition, which had kept the door slammed shut on Hawaii, melted in the final hours of House debate.

Speaker Rayburn, Texas Democrat, who once said the Statehood Bill would pass over his dead body, came over in the last hour.

Stocks Late
Because of transmission delay, the New York Stock Exchange quotations are not included in this edition.

Honolulu Star-Bulletin

HONOLULU, TERRITORY OF HAWAII, U. S. A., THURSDAY, MARCH 12, 1959

Honolulu Star-Bulletin, Vol. 48, No. 61   ★★★★   Phone 57-911

Special Radio, Phone Lines Flash News

Sirens, Bells Herald Statehood Arrival

The wail of civil defense sirens informed Honolulu area residents that Statehood long awaited had [illegible] ...

Shopping Center, Kalihi Shopping Center and in Pauna.

At 7:25 p.m. the international bonfire will be lit at Sand Island.

From 7:30 to 9 p.m. the Armed Forces will set off pyrotechnics off Leeward Oahu.

Tomorrow, legislators and other Government officials are scheduled to proceed from Iolani Palace at 9 a.m. to Kawaiahao Church, where an interdenominational service is to be held.

A joint concert by the Royal Hawaiian Band and Armed Forces bands is scheduled for 10 a.m. at the Palace.

At 11 a.m. a Statehood Commemoration Ceremony is to be held there.

At noon a 50-gun salute is to be fired from the Palace grounds. Simultaneously, Hawaii Air National Guard planes are to fly in formation over the legislative chambers. **Turn to Page 1-D, Column 7**

Faubus's Telegram

Statehood support and congratulations came from many sources, including areas in the Deep South from where they weren't expected.

As an example, the United Press released a telegram today sent by Governor Orval E. Faubus of Arkansas, undated but held up until Congress had completed action.

Governor Faubus's telegram reads:

"For years I have favored and have openly supported Statehood for both Hawaii and Alaska. Please accept my sincere congratulations on soon becoming the 50th State of the Union."

DIRECTORY

Bulletin Board	36
Business	19
Classified Ads	32-35
Comics	26
Editorials	6
Legislature	12
Obituaries	3
Society	22-23
Sport	28-31
Theatre Guide	25
TV-Radio	24

Islands in Transition

The idea of statehood for Hawaii originated well before World War II. Technically, statehood had been proposed as early as 1854 in an aborted treaty of annexation that contained a clause calling for eventual statehood. The notion began to be taken seriously by people outside Hawaii sometime in the early 1950's.

Certainly Hawaii deserved statehood.

Hawaii had been hammered on the anvil at Pearl Harbor. Over 30,000 of its young men and women had served in the armed forces during World War II. Hawaii's own special regiment, the 442nd, had won unparalleled battlefield honors. Ninety percent of Hawaii's people were full-fledged U.S. citizens and her population of half a million already outnumbered that of some of the states.

As early as 1948, the Democratic party included statehood for Hawaii in its campaign platform and the Republicans followed suit four years later. The Hawaii Statehood Commission lobbied actively year after year. Opposition to statehood came from a few southern Congressmen and Senators, assisted by certain conservative northern legislators. These opponents used every argument in the book. They claimed that Hawaii was a "non-contiguous" territory and had no place as a State. Hawaii was infested with more Communists than any other state in the Union; and so on. What this really meant was that many southern Democrats and conservative legislators of both parties were uncomfortable with the idea of an American state where the majority of citizens were not white and were expected to vote Republican to the detriment of the national political balance.

Unsuccessful statehood bills appeared in Congress in 1947, 1950 and 1953. Alaska was also petitioning to become a state and the admission of either or both states would change the prevailing situation in Congress vis-a-vis Democrats and Republicans. Finally, in 1958, Congressional Delegate Jack Burns, who later became Governor, recognized that if Democratic Alaska were allowed statehood first, then Congress would be willing to accept Republican Hawaii. In June, 1958, Alaska became the 49th State.

With the admission of non-contiguous Alaska, some remaining objections to Hawaiian statehood were removed. Congress finally voted statehood on March 12, 1959. After a plebiscite in which Hawaii's voters overwhelmingly approved statehood, Hawaii was admitted on August 21. Ironically, Jack Burns, who had done so much to bring statehood to Hawaii, was not invited to the signing of the proclamation in Washington, D.C.

The Honolulu Advertiser

John A. (Jack) Burns, who labored so mightily for statehood and who served as governor from 1962 to 1974. As champion of Japanese-American participation in island politics, he lived to see his protege, George Ariyoshi, become the nation's first Governor of Japanese ancestry.

The changing profile of Downtown Honolulu reflects its growing importance as the business and financial hub of the Central Pacific. Decisions made in these buildings spur economic activities in Fiji, New Guinea, Indonesia, Iran, Central and South America. "We have all too long thought of these glamorous islands as a legendary paradise rather than as a maturing international society which they in fact are." James A. Michener.

Photo

116

Islands in Transition

Although Hawaii has always been undergoing social change, the decade of the sixties and the early years of the seventies saw an unprecedented economic expansion. This growth, resulting from the coming of statehood and faster and larger airplanes, changed the entire complexion of the State's economic structure. As Hawaii accommodated itself to the burgeoning travel and leisure market of the mainland United States and Japan, tourism became its major industry; the importance of sugar and pineapple in the State's economy declined dramatically; and the island of Oahu, where over eighty percent of the State's population lives, became highly urbanized. By the 1990s, urbanization and resort development had spread to the former sugar fields of West Oahu, and a planned "second city" at Kapolei has emerged on Oahu's Ewa Plains. Population growth and resort development have also occurred on the Neighbor Isles, particularly on the Kohala Coast on the Big Island and the south and west sides of Maui.

There had been an earlier burst of economic activity during World War II when the enormous military build-up resulted in temporary increases in population, employment and construction. As a result of the wartime military presence, Hawaii's population zoomed from 428,000 persons in 1940 to 859,000 in 1944. But by 1950, with the military presence normalized, it plummeted to 498,000. Since then, the State's population has been steadily climbing, reaching 642,000 in 1960, and 774,000 in 1970. Today, Hawaii's resident population totals 1,165,500, with 1,050,700 local residents, 52,700 armed forces personnel and their 62,200 dependents. Additionally, on any given day, there are approximately 148,750 visitors present.

The rapid economic growth of the sixties and the early seventies was accompanied by an unprecedented boom in construction. New homes and apartment complexes, shopping centers, office buildings and public structures sprouted in what had previously been open spaces, mountain slopes, rain forests and marshes. It was a development process that saw suburban areas become part of the city and country towns become suburbs. It also brought unparalleled economic prosperity, visible almost everywhere in new housing, higher incomes, more cars, increased government services, a resurgence of downtown Honolulu, and a massive build-up of Waikiki. Almost overnight, Hawaii, which had known some hard economic times, particularly during the late forties, became one of the more well-to-do states in the Union.

However, there was infringement on Hawaii's precious environment. The sea, the coastal areas, the mountain slopes, the clean air, and the open plains were all imposed upon by a combination of inadequate planning and seemingly uncontrollable economic development. Fortunately, the people of Hawaii have now become aware of the inescapable tradeoffs between further economic prosperity and the natural environment. Plans for future growth are now carefully scrutinized by both the public and private sectors in regard to their social and environmental impacts. Interestingly, Hawaii has been the first state in the Union to pass a land use law.

During the 1980s, Japan's growing economy had a huge impact on Hawaii. The strength of the yen dramatically increased property acquisitions, real estate prices, taxes, and development. By the 1990s, Japan's economic recession, preceded earlier by the economic downturn caused by the Gulf War, slowed the growth of Hawaii's economy.

Since 1970 there has been a renaissance of interest in Hawaiiana, motivated by a genuine concern for the preservation of Hawaii's unique local culture, seemingly threatened by the disruptive effect of rapid economic expansion and the influx of new residents from the mainland states. Hawaiian language studies, Hawaiian crafts, and Hawaiian history are now more popular than ever, and *hula* classes are well attended throughout the Islands by all races. Parades, pageants and other events associated with Hawaii's many ethnic groups draw growing participation.

The islands of Hawaii are still in transition. A look into the crystal ball foresees continuation of Hawaii's multiculturalism. The Aloha State has one of the most unique blends in the U.S., in terms of variety of ethnicities living and not living here. While African-Americans make up more than 10% of the U.S. Mainland population, they are only 2.5% of Hawaii's population. Hispanic people are also underrepresented in Hawaii. On the other hand, almost half of the State's population is of Asian ancestry, from Japan, China, Korea, the Philippines or Vietnam. Hawaii is the only state where Caucasians are outnumbered by non-Caucasians and, as to be expected, the ratio of Hawaiians and other Pacific Islanders is also much higher in Hawaii. Intermarriage continues to shape the cosmopolitan character of Hawaii, with 31.1% of marriages in 1992 being interracial, and, if tourist marriages in Hawaii are not counted, nearly half of Hawaii's marriages are between people of different races.

As Hawaii adjusts to higher population and the development of the neighbor islands, hopefully the special qualities that make Hawaii unique will be left intact. That is the challenge facing Hawaii today.

The Hawaiian Renaissance

One of the most important political and social developments in recent Hawaii history has been the emergence of the Hawaiian Renaissance. It is expressed culturally with a renewed interest in Hawaiian art and traditions, including hula, music, history, literature and crafts; politically with demands for economic and social changes to correct past historical injustices; and socially with renewed pride and consciousness in being Hawaiian.

Quite effectively, this renewed interest has brought to a halt the melancholy decline of Hawaiian culture that had gone practically unabated for two hundred years. Since contact with the West began, the Hawaiian people have experienced the tragic consequences of massive population decline due to foreign diseases, loss of political and social power, and heavy influxes of non-Hawaiian peoples.

Hawaiian cultural revivals have happened before, though not on the scale that is now occurring. Under the encouraging leadership of King David Kalakaua, the hula and many other aspects of the ancient culture were rescued from near oblivion. When Kalakaua included sacred hulas and chants as part of his coronation celebrations, he shocked the stuffier members of Honolulu's society.

Kalakaua attempted a revival of native customs because of his sincere interest in the songs, chants, legends and dances of his people, considering them the expression of true nationhood. He was also very much aware of the declining Hawaiian participation in government, a condition brought on by the fact that Hawaiians were beginning to be outnumbered by non-Hawaiians and were becoming demoralized under the impact of western ways and the contempt with which the increasingly dominant foreigners looked upon the native culture.

Kalakaua recognized the need to instill a sense of pride in his people along with an appreciation for the accomplishments of their ancestors. He felt that, with this increased self respect, the Hawaiian people would once more assume their rightful place in governing their land and that the disastrous population decline might be reversed. One of the sad phenomena of Kalakaua's times was that so many Hawaiians seemed to have lost the will to survive, and their declining numbers were not being maintained, let alone increased, by a shockingly low birth rate. When Kalakaua died, his sister Liliuokalani attempted to continue the revival, but the overthrow of the Hawaiian monarchy shortly after she inherited the throne dealt this revival a near fatal blow.

Sporadic attempts at revival continued to be made thereafter, though they were usually restricted to a particular aspect of the ancient culture. Duke Kahanamoku, for example, stimulated a world-wide enthusiasm for Hawaii's true national sport, surfing, found nowhere else on earth until that time. Similarly a revival of outrigger canoe racing occurred in the early 1900's, when it had become an almost forgotten activity. There were also attempts at setting up Hawaiian cultural centers or villages where the ancient arts could be practiced along with a revival of the old way of life, such as Ulu Mau Village, which flourished during the 50's and 60's. Unfortunately such projects encountered public indifference.

The last decade or so has seen the most recent attempt at a Hawaiian Renaissance come into full bloom. It is hard to say what single event, if any, gave birth to the current renewal of interest. Certainly there has been some influence from similar movements on the mainland as well as a reaction to what many feel is excessive economic development and urbanization of the Islands. Perhaps like many other social movements, the Hawaiian Renaissance began because its time had come.

There is no doubt that the renaissance has become a force of growing importance in the Islands. Early on its political significance was felt. The Navy bombing of Kaho'olawe was scaled down and reparation bills were presented in Congress. Economic plans must now consider the rights of people to the land and incorporate a respect for the old rural lifestyle. In significant ways the Renaissance touches the lives of everyone who comes in contact with it. Many of the old values are being reappreciated and practiced again.

The Hawaiian Renaissance

Hula

After King Kalakaua's aborted revival of the ancient dances, hula tended to drift into a pallid imitation of itself - the kind of dance popular in nightclubs catering to tourists or the South Sea movies in which "authentic" blonde hula maidens danced in grass skirts made of cellophane strips. The Hawaiian Renaissance has helped to rescue this noble art form from degradation. Today the Islands are vibrating with the beat of serious hula schools where the key words are authenticity and discipline.

These schools are headed up by kumu hula (sources or masters of hula) and teach strict versions of the ancient sacred hulas and chants. This hula form is a rigorous discipline and only the most dedicated last very long. There has also been an upsurge of interest in men's hulas. In the olden days specific and very vigorous dances were performed only by men.

But such developments in no way represent a sterile and foredoomed attempt to revive a past which can never be totally recaptured. Hula was always a living and changing form. Modern masters of the hula and chant teach the old ways, the transitional styles of Kalakaua's time, and even incorporate the steps and changes introduced during the popularity of "tourist" hula in the 30's and 40's — all part of the history of Hawaii's national dance. It is good to know that the hula is alive, well, and growing — that it will continue to inspire wherever it is seen. The annual Merrie Monarch Festival, which is named in honor of His Majesty King Kalakaua, is held every April on the Big Island, and is Hawaii's top hula competition.

Robert E. Van Dyke Collection

Hula dancers at King Kalakaua's Jubilee Luau on his fiftieth birthday, November 16, 1886 on the grounds of Iolani Palace. Though aptly named "The Merrie Monarch" for his love of parties, King David Kalakaua had a deeply serious side to his nature. He was sincerely interested in preserving important elements of the ancient Hawaiian culture. The appearance of hula dancers at this luau was a calculated defiance of the missionary-dominated establishment of the time which, if it had its way, would have condemned the hula to extinction. Though frowned upon by many of the prominent families, some of whom refused to attend, these hula performances were a symbol of pride for the Hawaiian people and a sign that their ruler had the interests of his people at heart.

The Hawaiian Renaissance

Music

Auntie Genoa Keawe, one of the greats of Hawaiian music. She is famed for her falsetto renditions of the old classics and the sensitivity of her interpretations of Hawaii's songs.

Alexis Hi

Left: Eddie Kamae of the **Sons of Hawaii,** *prominent in Hawaiian music.*

Alexis Higdon

The Hawaiian Renaissance

Two decades ago Hawaiian music was considered to be a declining art form. There was a time when one could tune in to almost any Honolulu radio station and hear Hawaiian music. But by 1970 or thereabouts, only one station still consistently played Hawaiian music. Older musicians were not being replenished from the ranks of young musicians who were interested in, as were young people everywhere, rock music.

Today, the situation has turned almost completely around. Hawaii's younger people, particularly those of Hawaiian ancestry, now listen to and play Hawaiian music, coming to appreciate their own rich musical heritage, including the ancient chants, the "hapahaole" music of the 30's and 40's, and today's folk-oriented styles. *Reggae, the music of another island people, has become popular in Hawaii, where the Caribean beat is blended with Hawaiian music, called "Jawaiian" (a combination of the words "Jamaica" and "Hawaiian").*

Traditional Hawaiian instrumental music owes its unique sound to the slack-key guitar style. To this style, young Hawaiian musicians have added more instruments and some elements of standard popular music to derive a musical sound that is valid within the Hawaiian framework, but appealing to a wider audience. New songs reflect a yearning for the simplicity of a way of life now past, a love of the land, and a concern for what is being done to it.

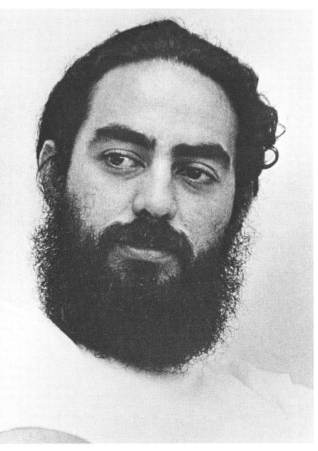

Alexis Higdon

George Helm, talented Hawaiian musician/ singer who became passionately involved with the issues of "aloha 'aina" (love for the land) and the misuse of Kaho'olawe. His mysterious disappearance at sea, while returning from Kaho'olawe to Maui on a surfboard after having searched for other activists who he feared were marooned there, was a sad loss to all Hawaiians whatever their feelings about Kaho'olawe. He was a sensitive, articulate and gentle man, deeply concerned about the future of these islands.

Right: Gabby Pahinui, one of the greats of today's Hawaiian music scene and a musical pioneer of the Hawaiian Renaissance.

Alexis Higdon

121

One of America's most unusual bicentennial projects was the voyage of Hokule'a, a replica of the ancient Polynesian double-hulled migration canoes that brought the first Polynesians to these islands more than a thousand years ago. The Polynesian Voyaging Society's project is especially fitting as Hawaii's contribution to the national bicentennial celebration because it symbolizes the uniqueness and exotic heritage of America's only oceanic state. Centuries before European settlers founded colonies on America's eastern shores, Hawaii's earliest settlers had mastered the navigation of the earth's largest ocean, bringing with them the full range of their domesticated plants and animals to start a new life in a new land.

Alexis H

The Hawaiian Renaissance

Hokule'a

Of all the recent manifestations of the Hawaiian Renaissance, no one event or object has had a more dramatic effect than the voyage of the *Hokule'a*, a replica of the ancient double-hulled migration canoes that brought the first Polynesian inhabitants to these islands a thousand years ago. Hokule'a means "star of gladness," the Hawaiian name often attributed to Arcturus, Hawaii's zenith star, which guided the sixty-foot-long canoe home after its successful voyage to Tahiti which began on May 2, 1976. Piloted by old Polynesian navigational methods, *Hokule'a* re-opened a highway on the sea once traveled by similar splendid vessels in the golden age of Polynesian voyaging.

Centuries before European settlers founded colonies on America's eastern shores, Hawaii's earliest pioneers had mastered the navigation of earth's largest ocean, bringing with them to Hawaii a wide range of domesticated plants and animals. The voyage of *Hokule'a* was, in a sense, a time machine, journeying into the past to recreate a saga as basic to the beginnings of Hawaii as the voyage of the *Mayflower* was to the founding of our nation.

Hokule'a and her crew of 17 arrived in Tahiti to a tumultuous welcome perhaps unrivalled in Tahiti's history. Twenty-five thousand or more Tahitians crowded the shoreline of Papeete's harbor to partake of the pride and accomplishment of their Hawaiian brothers. The magnificent sailing canoe returned to Hawaii to a joyous reception that saw masses of people cheering as she came in sight. This successful voyage reawakened a deep pride among Hawaiians in the accomplishments of their ancestors, a people who could build a giant ship using only wooden, bone and stone tools and then navigate it, employing only the stars and other natural signs as guides over the vast deep Pacific.

Hokule'a has become the visible symbol of everything encompassed in the words "Hawaiian Renaissance." After her return from Tahiti, *Hokule'a* was used as a floating classroom. Elementary and high school students were taken aboard to study how their ancestors coped with navigation and survival in an age when metal tools and electronic instruments were unknown. A planned second trip to Tahiti was aborted only five hours after departure on March 16, 1978, when the *Hokule'a* capsized in rough seas south of Molokai. One crewman was lost when he left the overturned ship in an attempt to swim to Lanai for help.

Nevertheless, the triumph of *Hokule'a* endures. Her maiden voyage stirred the imagination of people all over the world. By the mid-1990s the *Hokule'a* had completed five trans-Pacific voyages. On May 13, 1995, the *Hokule'a* finished its first voyage with a flotilla of Polynesian voyaging canoes. *Hokule'a* was joined by two other Hawaiian crafts, as well as a New Zealand Maori and two Cook Island canoes. The motorless boats successfully sailed from Tahiti and the Marquesas to Hawaii, using the techniques of wayfinding navigation. For the first time, one of the voyaging vessels, *Hawai'iloa*, was constructed primarily of traditional materials.

Tip Davis, Polynesian Voyaging Society

The Hokule'a on a training excursion before the voyage to Tahiti.

Alexis Higdon

When Hokule'a came to visit Hilo after her epic voyage to Tahiti and back, the turnout was enormous as Big Islanders flocked to welcome her. Here dancers perform ancient hulas in honor of the great ship, pride and joy of the native Hawaiian people.

Pam Smith

The garb of ancient Hawaii was long relegated to the limbo of night club shows and Aloha Week pageantry. Today, Hawaiians of all ages increasingly dress in the old style on ceremonial occasions and important gatherings to symbolize pride in their heritage.

124

The Hawaiian Renaissance

Aloha Aina (Love of the Land)

One unfortunate result of the Hawaiian's basic generosity of spirit, which viewed land as coming from the gods and as belonging to everyone to be used in trust, was that over the many decades most of Hawaii's most valuable land became separated from Hawaiian ownership. Hawaiians in the olden times had only a vague concept of private property, living as they did in a cooperative village social structure. Thus, it was easy for newcomers to "buy" land cheaply or to obtain ownership through compli-cated legal chicanery which the average man of those times neither understood nor cared about.

With political and social consciousness heightened by the Hawaiian Renaissance, it was inevitable that the question of reparation for the Hawaiian people be raised. Hawaiians had seen the land rights of American Indians and Native Alaskans recognized and compensation made for past injustices. Through the efforts of many Hawaiian organizations, a Hawaiian reparation bill is now under consideration in Congress.

KAHO'OLAWE

Kaho'olawe is a small, uninhabited island off Maui's southwest coast. From the air it looks like the kind of Polynesian island people dream about. In reality, it is dry, dusty and dangerous to walk upon because of enormous quantities of unexploded bombs and shells accumulated over decades of bombardment. Since World War II, it has been used by the U.S. Navy for target practice by both carrier airplanes and warships.

Its only permanent inhabitants are bands of hardy goats who doubtless have been the cause of much vegetative destruction due to their habit of cropping the already scanty vegetation too closely. It is felt that with the removal of the goats, the land could once again support a fairly dense cover of plant life adapted to its dry climate.

Archaeological investigation has revealed that the island had major religious and cultural importance and that it once supported a small permanent population. It has also been found that the island is rich in unusual sites and artifacts that will contribute much to our knowledge of periods of Hawaiian history that are presently a mystery. But years of bombing have endangered many of the ancient sites and have made the island a very hazardous place to visit. This seemingly destructive use of the land symbolizes to many a total contradiction of the concept of "Aloha Aina." As a result, the island has become a rallying point that calls attention to the continued abuse of Hawaii's limited land area. In 1990, President Bush ordered a moratorium on the bombing of Kaho'olawe. In 1993 Congress approved the return of Kaho'olawe to the State of Hawaii, along with a program to clean up unexploded bombs and reforest the barren, 45 square mile island. On May 7, 1994, the Federal government formally turned Kaho'olawe over to the State.

Alexis Higdon

Controversy hangs over Kaho'olawe as surely as the clouds in the photograph. The issue of "Aloha Aina" remains one of the most crucial social and political issues of the nineties and beyond. Because of the debate over Kaho'olawe, Hawaii had to address the important question of what is proper usage of all the land in Hawaii nei. Is land just another commercial commodity, or are there social and spiritual aspects to be taken into consideration? The way this question is answered will be of overwhelming importance for the future of Hawaii.

Hawaiian Sovereignty

By the late 1980s, the Hawaiian Renaissance had evolved into the Hawaiian Sovereignty movement. The quest for sovereignty which once seemed relegated to the lunatic fringe had become mainstream.

The defining moment for Hawaiian Sovereignty came in January 1993, during the "Onipa'a" commemoration marking the centennial of the overthrow of the independent Kingdom of Hawaii. (Onipa'a was Queen Liliuokalani's motto and means "steadfastness.") The largest political demonstrations in State history took place at Iolani Palace, with 16,000 Hawaiians and their supporters rallying to protest the 1893 U.S.-backed coup. The massive demonstrations included an open air, theatrical re-enactment of the overthrow. Then-Governor John Waihee, a Hawaiian, ordered the removal of American flags from the capitol district during the hundred-year anniversary observances.

The Onipa'a mobilization marked a paradigm shift in Hawaii's consciousness, and Hawaiian sovereignty came of age, becoming a political force to be reckoned with. President Bill Clinton signed a joint Congressional resolution apologizing to the Hawaiian people for the illegal overthrow and the U.S. role in it. Hawaiian activists held a tribunal that found America guilty of war crimes and genocide against the Kanaka Maoli (Hawaiian people). From then on, there was no turning back.

Beyond a general notion of Sovereignty as indigenous empowerment, the concept means different things to different parts of the Hawaiian community.

The nation-within-a-nation model, advocated by Kia Aina (governor) Mililani Trask of Ka Lahui Hawai'i (the Sovereign Nation of Hawaii), would give Hawaiians the same rights most other Native Americans currently have. There would be a tribunal reservation system tied to a land base and a sovereign Hawaiian entity that would have a government-to-government relationship with Washington. This entity would be Federally recognized as a nation-within-a-nation, with Hawaiians remaining U.S. citizens.

The state-within-a-state model, articulated by Office of Hawaiian Affairs Trustee Kina'u Boyd Kamali'i, would create a new super-Office of Hawaiian Affairs (the State agency now charged with oversight pertaining to indigenous matters). It could merge OHA, the Department of Hawaiian Home Lands, and

Elizabeth Pa Martin

Queen Lili'ukalani's statue overflows with floral ho'okupu which were reverently placed there by those who loved and cherished the Queen's memory and legacy at the five-day January 1993 Onipa'a commemoration of the January 17, 1893 overthrow of the Hawaiian monarchy.

other public and private Hawaiian entities into a political subdivision within the State government that would wield county-like power.

The most radical departure, advocated by activist attorney Hayden Burgess and Dennis "Bumpy" Kanahele of the Nation of Hawaii, is total independence, which would remove Hawaii from the Union and reestablish Hawaii as an independent nation-state, like the various members of the United Nations. Some within this departure favor democracy, others seek restoration of the monarchy.

A controversial State-sponsored referendum relating to Hawaiian Sovereignty is scheduled for late 1995. The hundredth anniversary of U.S. annexation in 1998 has the potential of once again rallying the Kanaka Maoli as 1993's Onipa'a commemorations did. The Hawaiian Sovereignty movement remains the wild card in State politics.

The Bishop Museum

Queen Liliuokalani sits in Washington Place surrounded by friends and family. Not surprisingly, she did not attend the annexation ceremony and the rising of the United States flag which officially ended her reign and the Kingdom of Hawaii that began with Kamehameha I.

Star Bulletin, Dennis Oda

One-hundred year later, the largest political gathering in Hawaii's history commemorates the overthrow and the events leading up to it in front of flag-draped Iolani Palace located in downtown Honolulu. From all the islands, from all walks of life, Hawaiians gathered in unity.

127

Bibliography

C. Brewer & Company, Ltd. *1974 Calendar.* Treasury of Ancient Hawaiiana.

Chinen, Jon. ·*The Great Mahele,* University of Hawaii Press, Honolulu, 1958.

Craighill Handy, E.S. and others. *Ancient Hawaiian Civilization,* C. E. Tuttle Co., Rutland, Vt., 1965.

Craighill Handy, E. S. and Pukui, Mary Kawena. *The Polynesian Family System in Ka'u, Hawaii,* C. E. Tuttle Co., Rutland, Vt., 1972.

Daws, Gavan. *Shoal of Time - A History of the Hawaiian Islands.* University of Hawaii Press, Honolulu, 1974.

Duncan, Arlene K., Editor. *All About Hawaii - Thrum's Hawaiian Almanac, Vol. 91,* SB Printers, Honolulu, 1974.

Feher, Joseph; Joesting, Edward; Bushnell, O.A. *Hawaii: A Pictorial History.* Bishop Museum Press, Honolulu, 1969.

Goodman, Robert B. *The Hawaiians,* Honolulu, Island Heritage Press, 1970.

Grosvenor, Gilbert M., Editor. *National Geographic Magazine, December 1974.* National Geographic Society, Washington, D. C., 1974.

Hawaii Department of Planning & Economic Development. *State of Hawaii Data Book,* Honolulu, 1977.

Kahanamoku, Duke - with Joe Brennan. ·*Duke Kahanamoku's World of Surfing.* Grosset & Dunlap, New York, 1968.

Kuykendall, Ralph S. *The Hawaiian Kingdom, 3 Vols,* University of Hawaii Press, Honolulu, 1966-1968.

Lind, Andrew W. *Hawaii's People,* University of Hawaii Press, Honolulu, 1967.

McLaughlin, Gary, Editor. *Your Navy in Hawaii - 1974,* Military Publishers, San Diego, California, 1974.

Mrantz, Maxine. *Hawaiian Monarchy - The Romantic Years,* Tongg Publishing Co., Ltd., Honolulu, 1974.

Multi-Cultural Center. *The Samoans in Hawaii,* Honolulu, 1973.

Nordyke, Eleanor C. *The Peopling of Hawaii,* University of Hawaii Press, Honolulu, 1977.

Pukui, Mary K. and Elbert, Samuel H. *Hawaiian Dictionary,* University of Hawaii Press, Honolulu, 1971.

Scott, Edward B. *The Saga of the Sandwich Islands.* Sierra-Tahoe Publishing Co., Crystal Bay, Lake Tahoe, Nevada, 1968.

Smith, Pam. *Hawaii Observer,* Honolulu, May 19, 1977.

The Ethnic Research and Resource Center. *The Portuguese in Hawaii - A Resource Guide,* Hawaii Foundation for History and the Humanities, Honolulu, 1973.

Vandercook, John W. *King Cane - The Story of Sugar in Hawaii,* Harper & Brothers, New York, 1939.

Wallin, Homer N. *Pearl Harbor: Why, How, Fleet Salvage and Final Appraisal,* Chapters 7-8, pp. 99-122, U.S. Naval History Division, 1968.

Zambucka, Kristin. *Princess Kaiulani,* The Last Hope of Hawaii's Monarchy, Mana Publishing Company, Honolulu, 1976.

NOTES ON THE ILLUSTRATIONS

5. Freycinet, Louis Claude de - Voyage autour du monde, fait par ordre du Roi, sur les corvettes l'Uranie et la Physicienne, pendant les annees 1817 a 1820. Paris, Pillet aine, 1824-44. 3 vols en 4 part. 4to, et Atlas Atlas folio de 112 plates.

6. Ellis, William - Authentic narative of a voyage performed by Capts. Cook and Clerke, during the years 1776-1780. London, 1782.

7. Unknown.

8. Choris, Louis - Voyage pitteresque autour du monde, effrant des portraits des sauvages d'Amerique, d'Asie, d'Afrique et du grand Ocean, leurs armes, habillements, parures, utensils . . . accompagnes de descriptions par M. le baron Cuvier, etc., le tout dessine par M. Louis Choris, dans le voyage qu'il a fait de 1815-1818: lithographie par luimene et d'autres artistes. Paris, Choris (imprim. de Firmin Didet), 1821-23. Folio 110 plates.

8. Arago, Jacques - Promenade autour du monde pendant les annees 1817-18-19 -20, sur les corvettes du roi L'URANIE et la PHYSICIENNE, commandees par M. Freycinet. Paris, Leblanc, 1823. 2 volumes in 8v0. et Atlas en folio de 26 plates.

8. Byron, Capt. Lord George A. - Narrative of the voyage of H. M. ship *Blonde* to the Sandwich Islands, in 1824-25, for the purpose of conveying the bodies of their late King and Queen to their native country. (With an introduction by Mrs. Maria Graham, also editor) London, John Murray, 1827. 4to pages 260, plates and maps. Drawings by Dampier.

9. Cook, (Capt. James) - A voyage to the Pacific Ocean, undertaken by command of His Majesty, for making discoveries in the Northern hemisphere: performed under the direction of Captains Cook, Clerke and Gore, on H. M. ships *Resolution* and *Discovery,* in the years 1776-1780. Volume I and II written by Capt. James Cook: Volume III by Capt. James King. Published by order of the Lords Commissioners of the Admiralty. London, 1784. 3 volumes in 4to. 1 volume folio of 87 plates.

10. Cook, Capt. James - Same as page 9.

11. Cook, Capt. James - Same as page 9.

12. Cook, Capt. James - Same as page 9.

13. Cook, Capt. James - Same as page 9.

14. Kotzebue, Otto von - Entderkungs-Reise in der Sud See und nach der Behring's Strasse, in den Jahren 1815-1818. Weimar, Hoffmann, 1821. 3 volumes 4to. Figures and maps.

16. An interpretive drawing made into a photograph by the early Photographic firm of Williams and Co. of Hawaii.

18. Kamehameha II, from a drawing on stone lithographed by Hayter of London,1825.

20. See page 8; same description as this drawing by Dampier.

58. Description same as page 8.

59. Description same as page 8.

Index